Mastering Grammar

The SUM of All Those Errors: Syntax, Usage, and Mechanics

CAROLE LOFFREDO

authorHOUSE®

AuthorHouse™
1663 Liberty Drive
Bloomington, IN 47403
www.authorhouse.com
Phone: 1-800-839-8640

Published by AuthorHouse   08/25/2012

ISBN: 978-1-4685-8425-7 (sc)
ISBN: 978-1-4685-8423-3 (hc)
ISBN: 978-1-4685-8424-0 (e)

Library of Congress Control Number: 2012906887

TABLE OF CONTENTS

DEDICATION

This book is dedicated with love to my former students
who have lost their notes
and
to my beloved grandchildren Max and Jesse
so they don't have to write them.

PREFACE

If you are a new teacher or, as sometimes happens, you are a science or math teacher who must teach language arts or even a language arts teacher but overwhelmed with the task, I am writing this book for you.

Unfortunately, many schools offer no curriculum or a bad one, no support, no mentor. Many teachers are given only one or two courses in language arts in college. The assumption seems to be that if one can write at all, he/she can teach that skill. Teachers find themselves, pretty much, in a sink or swim situation, and before very long, about half of them sink and choose other careers. *Mastering Grammar* is an outline for direct instruction of basic language arts editing skills to use until you are comfortable enough "to do your own thing" or to make sense of a curriculum guide.

This book can also just as easily be used by any person who needs to improve his/her writing and speaking skills. The best way to learn something is to teach it to someone else. As you read the material, play both parts: teacher and student.

My teaching career spanned thirty-five years because I had the good fortune of working with Glenn Camp, the finest of principals. Because of his leadership and support, I continued teaching—unlike so many of us who leave the profession. When I first began teaching, I was hired with eleven other English teachers, and after six years, only I remained. Then I quit to be a full time mom and to care for my new family. I returned to teaching after eight years, somewhat reluctantly, and then worked with Glenn. He displayed a trust in his staff to allow that creative license, so missing in today's schools, which permitted teachers to pursue excellence not only in their students but in themselves. I sorely missed him when he retired.

I was also blessed with my co-teacher Jan Blanas. Together we mastered the SUM and much more. Her commitment to excellence, unwavering support, and exemplary work ethic made teaching a joyful experience. Much of Jan is in this material.

On a less personal note, but with much gratitude, working with Camille Blackowicz, a brilliant professor at National-Louis University, provided me with the understanding of vocabulary developing along a continuum. She taught me how to teach reading, a skill missing in the preparation for high school English teachers.

After so many years, degrees, additional classwork, and workshops, it is impossible to acknowledge which individual provided what new knowledge, but much of what shaped me professionally is found in the sources mentioned at the end of the text.

I am also indebted to my students. They taught me, and many of their ideas are in this material. They spoiled me for many years; we had fun together. I miss them.

Finally, my deepest gratitude goes to my family who always supported me. Teaching demands many more hours than those in the classroom, and my family shared me without complaint. Even today, my grandchildren understand that Gramma took a little time to write a book.

The SUM of All Those Errors

The part of teaching effective writing (which everyone hates) is addressing all of the mistakes. Developing editing skills is an essential part of good writing and the core of placement tests, but teachers who mark papers to inform students of their errors are now viewed as prehistoric dinosaurs dripping blood (their red pens) as they attack the poor student. An effective teacher is not damaging egos when he/she helps a student understand the reasons for the marks, and that more often than not, the frequency of marks in the paper is the result of the same mistake.

A typical scenario for a grammar lesson is to read the lesson aloud with the class, discuss the examples, assign the lesson, check and grade the lesson with the class, and then move on to the next. The problem is that students can read a rule, such as, "A pronoun agrees with its antecedent in person, number, and gender," and not know what any of those words mean. These same students can do the exercises fairly well because they speak the language rather well. They only miss one or two sentences and are happy with their 80% or 90%. Unfortunately, these missed sentences are not mastered, yet they are the ones on placement tests and represent the errors that occur in the students' writing.

Another typical practice in language arts instruction is to fill time with worksheets on various grammatical problems. This approach is very prevalent with newer teachers because they have been taught that direct instruction in grammar is ineffective, and they themselves have had little training. In this approach the information is haphazard and lacks any sense or connection to writing and becomes the least effective method while reinforcing the belief that grammar instruction is a waste of time.

Peer editing is another popular approach in which students discuss each other's writing to discover and correct errors. Peer editing has its place but is an inefficient method because it does not guarantee coverage of problems. For example, students are tested on appositives, but how many students' writing samples contain them? And sadly, peer editing can become an exercise in the blind leading the blind while the teacher sits at his/her desk. If any of these approaches sound familiar, this is why grammar instruction is failing.

How does one effectively teach all of those errors? By direct instruction and chunking! There is an immense difference in handing out worksheets and covering grammar in a haphazard fashion and doing worksheet practice after direct instruction and chunking. Following direct instruction, group work becomes a scavenger hunt, a game to find the errors, and the students now have mental lists of the "treasures" to acquire and edit.

In order to chunk the information, the teacher has to have mastery of the editing skills, an understanding of the specific errors that occur on placement tests or in students' writing, and a method of delivery. In other words, the teacher must master the SUM of all those errors. The SUM addresses only the editing part of the writing process, not revision, and certainly no other aspects of the product. Yet make no mistake, the lack of that editing skill is what wrecks a paper and costs most students high marks on SAT and ACT placement tests. And, like what I say or not, the reason mastery seems to elude most students is because no one, neither teacher nor student, likes the drill.

I would argue that all teachers should understand their language, and although K-5 teachers would not necessarily directly teach the SUM to their pupils, they should have mastery of the information themselves because they are then aware of internal structures within their students' own language as well as the external structures in the reading material they are encountering. The task of raising scores and developing more mature writing falls on the middle school teachers. Middle school students can and should master this material prior to high school. The system underestimates what the sixth to eighth grader can learn and bores them with repetition of material ineffectively and repeatedly delivered. What this book offers is a method of delivery for mastering editing skills with the purpose of raising test scores and improving the editing aspects of writing with the added bonus of empowerment that results from the confidence of knowing that what one says and writes is "correct."

The acronym SUM is the name of the framework for chunking the editing skills. It also serves as a mnemonic device to recall the steps for editing one's writing. As students embark on the scavenger hunt for all of those errors in a writing selection, theirs or others, they are searching for the SUM: syntax, usage, and mechanics. The term *grammar* is ambiguous because it conjures up different definitions for students. For some students, grammar means punctuation or mistakes. Others think of that noun "stuff." In order to create an effective method of instruction, teachers must agree on the terminology. Therefore, it is better to avoid the word *grammar* and use more specific terminology.

S: Syntax means word order in sentence structure. Although understanding sentence structure certainly improves writing by increasing sentence variety, with respect to editing, the focus is only on structural errors including fragments, run-ons, and comma splices. When students understand sentence structure, they are better able to identify these structural errors and are not dependent on some intuitive understanding common in verbally talented students. Understanding syntax also improves the comprehension of the usage and mechanic rules in English that are covered later. The correct use of the expression *you and I* as opposed to *you and me* makes perfect sense if the speaker/writer understands the difference between a predicate noun and a direct object. A mechanics rule stating to use a comma in a compound sentence does not make sense if the student does not know what a compound sentence is.

U: Usage technically refers to such problems as when to say *less than* or *fewer*. (*Less than* for quantities like sand; *fewer* for items one can count like oranges.) However, texts lump many errors under the usage heading, and in this method, these errors are chunked into four categories: pronoun errors, subject-verb agreement errors, verb errors, and modifier errors. Notice how dependent these problems are on syntax! How does a student correct subject-verb agreement if he or she cannot find the subject and verb in a sentence? Teachers argue students acquire good usage by good modeling and practice. Good modeling and practice, over time, accomplish the goal—for good students. Unfortunately, most students, and even very good students, are now practicing, voraciously, as they text in substandard English.

M: Mechanics chunks punctuation and capitalization errors. Most students are overwhelmed by these rules because they view them the same way they do spelling. There seem to be too many variables and exceptions and no end to them. In fact, by the time a child reaches middle school, the number of rules needed for improved scores and reduced errors is a finite, very manageable number. Then, by chunking and connecting these rules to syntax, the underlying sentence structure, real comprehension and mastery become possible.

Higher test scores and improved editing skills in writing are dependent on understanding sentence structure. It is time to teach that basic skill again. Begin with syntax, the analysis of what a sentence actually is, and many problems in writing correct themselves, and later, the revision skill of sentence variety is more easily addressed and achieved.

Introducing the
Syntax Unit

How a teacher ultimately introduces or teaches a lesson is dependent on that teacher's creativity. The following models lead to mastery of the concept, but what a teacher adds or deletes after that mastery depends on his/her situation. I begin the syntax unit with a reference to the film, *Karate Kid*. Although some students may not have seen the film, with today's technology, a clip of the scene would introduce the unit. Using a film clip is a more palatable introduction than, "Open your books to the chapter on nouns." The scene is between Mr. Miyagi and Daniel. Daniel wants to learn karate, and as Mr. Miyagi is tying Daniel's headband, he explains that if Daniel wants to learn karate, he must do everything that Mr. Miyagi says. No questions, no arguments. Isn't this the tacit agreement between every coach and player, every teacher and student, every mentor and learner? Teachers always learn from their students, but first they teach. There are endless examples to choose: *Rocky, Hoosiers,* etc. I tell my students at the end of the clip that we do not have time for explanations, arguments, etc. They must do what I tell them to do, when I tell them to do it, and the way I tell them to do it, and in the end, they will master the task, and all questions will be answered. Point out to the students Daniel's frustration and discontentment with waxing on and waxing off. It is a long way from the noun "stuff" to good writing; it is work and may not initially make sense to them, but you are Miagi, and the process is nonnegotiable. If you are using this book as a student, then the same goes for you, my reader. If you keep thinking, this doesn't work or do not follow the process, then the method will fail. You must trust the teacher, agree to our "contract," (just as Daniel does) and then proceed.

Learning syntax is like working a jigsaw puzzle. How do you do a jigsaw puzzle? What is the first thing you do? You look at the picture. In learning syntax, you need to know what the picture is. Where are you headed?

You are after a real understanding of what a sentence is. Students, most students, know when they write a sentence or not, but they do not know how to define it. They really do not understand its structure. Therefore, the overall goal is to comprehend sentence structure. The picture is the sentence. If you cannot explain what a sentence is, then there is something to learn.

What is the next step when you work a jigsaw puzzle? You put the pieces into categories: the edges and the various colors. You apply the same strategy with the pieces of a sentence. You must arrange the pieces into categories to form a framework for study, a framework for the sentence. We will call this framework of the elements of syntax The Chart. The Chart is the foundation for mastering syntax. (Appendix I)

The framework model is based on Bloom's Taxonomy, the original version. Bloom's Taxonomy functions as the theoretical model of the learning process and as a means for students to measure their own learning and progress. The levels are knowledge, comprehension, application, analysis, synthesis, and evaluation. Students begin, of course, at the beginning level of knowledge. I firmly believe that one of the most flawed directions in education is the idea that memorization is a waste of time and the lowest form of learning. Students who are memorizing information are not engaged in levels of higher thinking, and that concern leads to the erroneous conclusion, therefore, that memorization is wrong. I would argue, however, that memorization is a necessary step to build the foundation for the development of higher thinking in any discipline. Over thirty-five years, I have observed students who have difficulty in math because they have not memorized number facts. Gifted students often have trouble because they have never had to memorize information and lack the discipline to do so when they finally encounter the task. Isn't a memorized alphabet the beginning of learning to read and write a language? In fact, isn't everything we know really what's remembered or in other words, memorized?

Learning syntax begins as a vocabulary lesson requiring memorization. By memorizing the vocabulary, students and teacher are beginning to develop a common terminology to later apply to all subsequent language discussions and writing. The approach to this vocabulary development is based on the theory that vocabulary progresses along a continuum. (Blackowicz) The following chart illustrates this progression and serves as the means for teacher and students to measure progress. (Appendix II)

The continuum consists of four levels. In Level I, the students knows the term and can correctly spell it. In Level II, the student learns the definition of each term. In Level III, the student identifies the terms in given sentences. In Level IV, students give their own examples of each term in sentences.

Mastering the framework builds the necessary foundation for learning syntax. These terms are just vocabulary words along the continuum. An entire universe is built on slightly more than ninety elements; the infinite varieties of sentence structure are built on slightly more than thirty syntactic structures. I am aware that memorizing the definitions does not mean comprehending them and that learning syntax does not mean good writing. We are talking about the beginning steps in a process—only. However, real comprehension depends on knowing vocabulary. For example, ask students what a fraction is or what pi is. They will give you an example of a fraction such as ¼ or say 3.14159 . . . . Only the very best student can define the terms.

Defining *noun* is the best way to illustrate the continuum chart and the progression through the thirty or so terms. Ask the class, "What is a noun?"

Almost unanimously the class will respond, "A person, place, or thing."

To which you respond, "No. That is incorrect. It is a good thing we are working together."

The class will throw a fit, protest loudly, and decide that you are incompetent. They will also listen, eager to prove you wrong. Ignore this and remind them you are Miyagi, the syntax master. To learn the chart, they will master each term like noun. First they must know the term. Everyone in the class has already done that. They know it, and they can spell it. Encourage them. Level I is completed.

Now they must master Level II on the continuum, the definition. They must "unlearn" *person, place, or thing*, and substitute that a noun names. What is a noun? A noun is a word or group of words occupying a slot in a sentence pattern that names. For the moment, students only have to learn what a noun does in a sentence. What is the definition of a noun? Names.

Now, students proceed to Level III. They must identify a noun in a sentence. In the sentence, "The dog barked," the students identify *dog* as the noun because *dog* is the word that names not because *dog* is a thing.

Finally, they are on Level IV. Real comprehension means a student can provide an example of the term. They will be able to use a noun in a sentence without difficulty. **Being able to give an example of all of the terms in the chart is the objective of the unit.** They have already finished one term. Review. Students have now completed an example of how the continuum works and how they are to approach each term for real, lasting comprehension. They are ready to begin Level I of The Chart.

The objective of Level I is to memorize all of the terms in the chart. They must memorize the entire chart in order with every term spelled correctly. They are not concerned with definitions, only the terms in the correct order and spelled correctly. Remind them that they are building the framework: the categories and colors in a language jigsaw puzzle. They are only at the knowledge level of Bloom's Taxonomy, and they are not working on definitions and comprehension until they are comfortable with just knowing the words. They have never even heard the word *participle* and have to learn to say it and read it before they can understand it.

At this point many readers are saying it can't be done and it is a waste of time and weaker students especially cannot do it. This attitude is why it won't work. For those of you still reading, you must go through the process as well as the students. It is unacceptable even unforgiveable that there are teachers who do not read the novels they assign, do not understand the exercises they assign, use answer keys to survive the day, etc. Be like your students and master each step one by one. You will better appreciate their struggle and also be able to anticipate difficulties. The first step is to be able to recite this chart without hesitation. Have the students in rows (a somewhat sinful practice nowadays), and assign each row one part of the chart. Then rotate rows. Oral drills rather than writing out the terms is most effective. Stronger students will learn the terms first, although they will have had to work for the first time in their academic careers. As each student learns the terms, make that student the teacher of a small group. You now have more time to work with any students having difficulty.

The following game is one way to teach the terms. I think it important to reiterate that rote memorization is of no value by itself. The memorization of the chart is just the first step in creating the knowledge base of Bloom's Taxonomy. If a student has never heard the word, participle, we cannot expect an evaluation of its use in a sentence, whether to correct his/her writing or to enhance it or to evaluate someone else's use of the term.

THE GAME

Give each student twelve 3 x 5 index cards. Fold the cards into thirds and cut. Copy the terms of the chart on the front of the cards. Check every card for misspellings so the students do not study inaccurate information. Provide a zip lock bag to hold the cards.

The next step can be confusing because the students are not creating the typical flashcard. **The definitions for the terms are NOT on the back of the term card, but on the back of the card across from it.** Lay the first two rows of the chart alongside of each other. Remove the verb card and the interjection card from Parts of Speech. These are two parts of speech but are not included in this game because the two rows will not line up. It is not necessary to study the definition of the verb card because the same definition occurs twice, and the interjection is not a significant concern with sentence structure, but students need to know there are eight parts of speech not six.

The rows are as follows:

Parts of Speech	Parts of a Sentence
noun	subject
pronoun	verb (predicate)
conjunction	direct object
preposition	indirect object
adjective	predicate noun
adverb	predicate adjective

Note that all predicates are verbs, but not all verbs are predicates. The term predicate refers to the job that a verb does in a sentence, but since all predicates are comprised of one to four verbs, students will label predicates as verbs. You must keep reminding students, however, that as they mark the verb in a sentence that they are marking the predicate. This adjustment will make more sense later. It is convenient to label the predicate as a verb to learn syntax, but on placement tests, students are asked to identify the predicate. They need to realize they are being asked to identify the verb(s).

Next the students write the definition of each term on the back side of the card opposite it. For example, the definition of a noun goes on the back of the subject card. So the back of the subject card says, "names." The back of the verb card says, "takes the place of a noun." (Notice that the definitions are actions explaining the job the term does in a sentence. For example, nouns name, verbs show or link, etc.) The back of the direct object card says, "joins words, phrases, and clauses." The back of the indirect object card says, "shows a relationship between a noun or pronoun and the rest of the sentence." The back of the predicate noun card says, "modifies nouns and pronouns." (Be certain to define the word modify as a word that is effecting some change on another word.) Finally, the back of the predicate adjective card says, "modifies verbs, adjectives, and other adverbs."

The back of the noun card has the definition for a subject, which says, "who or what does the action or is linked." On the back of the pronoun card is the definition for a verb (predicate) which says, "shows action or links." The back of the conjunction cards says, "receives the action." The back of the preposition card says, "receives the direct object." The back of the adjective card says, "follows a linking verb and renames the subject." The back of the adverb card says, "follows a linking verb and describes the subject."

To play the game, students begin with Level I by learning the terms one column at a time. They proceed through each column until they can lay out the entire chart. When they can write the terms, spelled correctly and in order, they proceed to Level II and learn the definitions.

To begin Level II, students learn the definitions for Parts of a Sentence first, not Parts of Speech. They gather up the terms for Parts of Speech and turn them over to line up and match the definitions for Parts of a Sentence. If necessary, they only do two terms at a time until they build to all six. After they know the Parts of a Sentence definitions, they reverse the process and turn the Parts of a Sentence terms over to match the definitions for Parts of Speech. Initially, the students will be confused (as you may be at this point), but once they actually start to work with the cards, they enjoy the learning and gain confidence in their ability to master the material. The game offers a quick check for the teacher of students' progress, and students can race with one another and work independently, in pairs, or in groups. They can also work at home with a copy of the chart as a substitute teacher while they practice with the cards. Parents can also help.

After students complete the first two columns and are beginning to understand how the game works, proceed to the next two columns: Phrases and Clauses. Unlike the first two categories of Parts of Speech and Parts of a Sentence, the actual category names of Phrases and Clauses have definitions. Therefore, students will write definitions on the back of the category cards as well as the other terms. Students lay out the next two rows. On the back of the Clause card, write, "a group of words." On the back of the independent card, write, "prep + noun." On the back of the dependent card, write, "a verb that acts like a noun, adjective, or adverb." On the back of the noun dependent clause card, write, "acts like an adjective." On the back of the adjective dependent clause card, write, "to + a verb, acts like a noun, adjective, or adverb." On the back of the adverb dependent clause card, write, "ends in ING and acts like a noun." Turn the cards over, and then write the definitions of Clauses on the back of the cards in the Phrase column. On the back of the Phrase card, write, "a group of words with a subject and a verb." On the back of the prepositional card, write, "a complete thought." On the back of the verbal card, write, "an incomplete thought." On the back of the participle card, write, "acts like a noun." On the back of the infinitive card, write, "acts like an adjective." On the back of the gerund card, write, "acts like an adverb." Now these columns are completed, and students work on these definitions.

A trick for learning the verbals is to use the acronym PIG. Chant the terms: participle, infinitive, gerund. Grunt, snort, whatever it takes. Only linguists and crazy English teachers think syntax is fun. The creative teacher must devise some means to convince the reluctant masses that they love syntax as well!

The last category of the chart is Sentence Types. For these two columns, take three blank cards and lay them beside the three sentence types. (Most texts mention a fourth sentence type, the compound-complex sentence, but then, we are only talking about combinations. It is not necessary to address a fourth type.). There is no definition for the category. On a blank card, write the definition across from the simple sentence card that says, "one independent clause." On the second blank card, lay it across from the compound sentence, and write, "two or more independent clauses." On the third blank card across from the complex sentence card, write, "at least one independent and one dependent clause." The backs of the Sentence Type cards are blank.

Play with the cards. Have contests. Give prizes. Begin with Level I in the vocabulary continuum. When everyone is able to write the terms in the chart, spelled correctly and in the correct order, it is time to proceed to Level II, the definitions. Remember this is just like a vocabulary test and not some insurmountable task. This chart is just a bare bones skeleton, but it's everything a student needs to know. You are not going to be adding more and more to it. If you happen to know syntax, think about how "grammar" is usually taught. There is no end to the terminology. Think about that noun. Texts and teachers try to account for every detail: concrete, abstract, proper, tangible, and intangible for nouns. Verbs are worse: state of being, intransitive, transitive, linking, helping, auxiliary, etc. Take heart. Most of this terminology can be scrapped. None of these terms are necessary in this method. We are not trying to be linguists, and we are not trying to describe nor account for all aspects of language and every sentence. We are only after a basic understanding of how a two-year-old learns to put a sentence together and how a young adult augments the same.

One of the reasons that teaching syntax does not work is that in the name of being correct or thorough, texts get too complicated, involved, and boring. Studying transitional or generative grammars is also off track. The Chart is a bare bones combination of linguistics and traditional instruction chunked so a student can swallow it. All of the necessary definitions are there, and the hard part is over. Naysayers are thinking that, "Yes, a student will learn what *surreptitious* means on Friday, but forget it by Monday." True, but students will keep using *these* terms throughout the rest of the instruction. The definitions begin to make sense in a larger picture as the comprehension of how the parts work develops, and that is real learning. Remember that students can say that a noun is a person, place, or thing, but cannot explain how that noun functions in a sentence. The rote memorization is an essential step which cannot be skipped, but once the rote memorization of terms and definitions is complete, students can begin real comprehension. They must, however, begin with Parts of a

Sentence not Parts of Speech because the concept of Parts of Speech is really more abstract than the traditional text approach can teach. Understanding a sentence means understanding patterns, and patterns are represented by Parts of a Sentence.

Consider the sentence, "Running is fun." Ask a student to identify the verb. They will tell you, "Running." But, *running* is the noun in the sentence. Isn't *running* the *name* of the activity? Seeing the position in the sentence and seeing that nouns fill certain slots in our sentence patterns is real comprehension of how nouns work. They are not persons, places, and things. Follow this design and trust me. Expect your students to trust you. When students begin to really learn and understand (the light bulb burns at last), you have given them a tool for life.

After students finish Levels I and II, they are ready to proceed to Level III of the continuum. Now the task is to identify the syntactic structures in given sentences and to analyze simple sentence patterns.

There are five basic patterns to sentence structure. One can build a case for more patterns. For example, in the sentence, "I am in the park," the pattern would be S (subject) + V (predicate) + adverb in some grammars. Another example would be, "I painted the barn red." What does one do with red? The purpose of this method is to create a tool for correcting errors and creating sentence variety. Accounting for every possible scenario, or trying to account for them, since no grammar is perfect, is not the point and is unnecessary. To achieve the objective, students need only understand the five patterns.

These five patterns are subject plus a verb labeled S+V; a subject plus a verb plus a direct object, S+V+DO; a subject plus a verb plus an indirect object plus a direct object, S+V+IO+DO; a subject plus a verb plus a predicate noun, S+V+PN; or a subject plus a verb plus a predicate adjective, S+V+PA. There are predicate pronouns, but then we are just switching parts of speech. Frankly, students really do not need to differentiate between PN (predicate nouns), PP (predicate pronouns), or PA (predicate adjectives). What matters is that they recognize the function of a predicate "something" as opposed to a direct object. Knowing the difference between these two complements (direct objects and predicate "somethings") does matter and affects later instruction in usage problems.

Students will mark Sentence Parts above the words being identified. Parts of a Sentence are marked above the words to show the pattern. Parts of Speech are below the words to show how these parts of speech function in the sentence. The lost art of diagramming sentences is actually beneficial as a visual for students to conceptualize that parts of speech are really positions or slots in a sentence pattern. The disadvantages of diagramming are that in more complicated sentences it is difficult to read the sentence back in its correct order and teachers/students get caught up in the diagram rather than the meaning. The dog ate the bone. <u>The dog|ate|the bone</u>. The slots are S|V|DO.

S + V + DO
Dog ate bone.
  n   v   n

With this method of labeling the Sentence Parts and the Parts of Speech, the sentence stays intact.

In this method the dialogue between the teacher and student differs from the traditional method so I am providing the dialogue. It is important that instruction using the questioning technique is followed exactly and consistently because this method imitates the way the child hears and then repeats a sentence. The brain receives the pattern in a given order so the analysis needs to match that order. Additional background information is in parentheses.

To begin Level III, write the first sentence on the board.

The pitcher balked.

Teacher: What is the action or link in the sentence? (Always begin with the verb and always use the definition. In this sentence, *balked* is the verb. Remember it is the predicate of the sentence, but we are calling it a verb in order to label it. Up to four verbs can make a predicate. For example, "The pitcher *should have been watching* first base." *Should have been watching* is the predicate composed of the four verbs: *should, have, been,* and *watching*. And once again, all predicates are verbs; later we will see that all verbs are not predicates. Do not label all four verbs but just the slot as the verb location.)

T: Remember we are building a pattern. We are identifying one of five patterns. We find the pattern by identifying the verb first and then the subject. We do this by asking questions based on the definitions. In the sentence, "The pitcher balked," what is the action or link?

Class: *Balked.*

T: Now create a question by combining the words *who or what* and the verb. For example, "Who or what balked?" The <u>answer</u> to the question is the <u>subject</u> of the sentence. Who or what balked?

C: Pitcher.

T: What are we doing?

C: Building a pattern. (They will not be able to answer this question yet, but will in time.)

T: We are building a pattern. What is the pattern?

C: S + V.

T: Great. Remember we are building patterns. You are identifying one of the five patterns and have completed the first one. Always find the pattern by identifying the verb first and then the subject by asking the same questions in the same order. (Students only need to label the single word at this point that identifies the basic sentence part. This pattern is also called the kernel of a sentence.)

      S   +   V

The pitcher balked.

You are now ready for the second pattern.

The pitcher threw the ball.

T: What is the action or link in the sentence? (Ultimately, of course, you are working for student independence and you would stop prompting them.)

C: *Threw.*

T: What is the question? (When they formulate the question, they always read the rest of the sentence following the verb. The rest of the sentence in these simple patterns is called the complete predicate. For testing, students need to be able to identify a complete predicate, but the purpose here is to keep the pattern in tact to facilitate comprehension.)

C: Who or what threw the ball? *Pitcher*; therefore, pitcher is the subject of the sentence.

T: What is the pattern so far?

C: S + V.

T: To continue identifying the pattern, you must learn to make a new question to locate the direct object if there is one. (This is a crucial part of the method. Students are not to ask what gets the action. Wording the question in this manner determines the choice based on what the student understands the sentence to mean, not what follows to build a pattern. Students must finish the pattern in their heads, the same way the brain receives the information. After determining the verb, students form the next question by saying the subject, the verb, and the word *what*. They say, "The pitcher threw what?" They can only say the subject and verb and the word *what*. Consider the sentence, "The boy went home." Students want *home* to be the direct object because it is a noun and in the right position in the sentence. In their minds they think where the boy went, and the answer is home. However, if they apply the correct question, "The boy went what?" The question does not make any sense. It does not make sense because there is no direct object in this sentence. *Home* is a noun, but it functions in the sentence as an adverb explaining where the boy is. Home does not receive any action from the verb *went*. One cannot went a home.)

T: Say the subject and the verb only and the word *what?* The pitcher threw what?

C: The pitcher threw what? *Ball*; therefore, *ball* is the direct object because it receives the action of being thrown.

T: What is the pattern?

C: S + V + DO

   S   +   V + DO
The pitcher threw the ball.

Now students are ready for the third pattern.

The pitcher threw the catcher the ball.

T: (Call on a student to analyze the sentence structure. Use the word *analyze*.)Sam, analyze the sentence, "The pitcher threw the catcher the ball."

Sam: The verb is *threw.* (Sam may begin with "The subject is *pitcher."* Some students will give the verb first or the subject first. Both responses are incorrect because they are just learning. Usually no one begins by following the steps in the method. They are always trying to be correct and give the right answer, but you are **not** after the answer, but the **method** of getting there. They do not understand, at first, that you want them to model the process.)

T: Who wants to help Sam?

Sam's friend: Because we always begin our analysis with locating the verb and use our definitions, the action or link in the sentence is *threw.* Therefore, *threw* is the verb. The next question to ask is, "Who or what threw the catcher the ball?" The answer is *pitcher;* therefore, *pitcher* is the subject. The important step now is to say the subject and the verb together followed by the word *what.* The pitcher threw what? The answer to the question is *ball;* therefore, *ball* is the direct object because the ball receives the action of being thrown. (Sam's friend has an IQ of 140. The objective is to get Sam and the class to model the process together.)

T: What is the pattern so far?

C: S + V + DO

T: Now use your definitions and ask, "What receives the direct object?"

C: Catcher. Therefore, *catcher* is the indirect object because it receives the direct object *ball.*

T: What is the pattern?

C: S + V + IO + DO

    S + V + IO + DO
The pitcher threw the catcher the ball.

T: The mother gave the baby a bottle. Analyze the sentence, class. (Or go back to Sam if he is ready.)

Sam: The action or link in the sentence is *gave.* Therefore, *gave* is the verb. Who or what gave the baby the bottle?. *Mother;* therefore, *mother* is the subject. The mother gave what? *Bottle;* therefore, *bottle* is the direct object because it receives the action of being given. Who or what receives the bottle? *Baby;* therefore, *baby* is the indirect object because baby receives the bottle, the direct object.

T: What are we trying to do?

C: Build a pattern.

T: What is the pattern?

C: S + V + IO + DO.

S   +   V   +   IO   +   DO

The mother gave the baby a bottle.

T: Notice in the pattern, S+V+IO+DO, the indirect object precedes the direct object. There is no indirect object without a direct object, and this is the pattern in English. Also, by definition, to have a direct object, the verb must be action. (At this point you might explain that the syntax or patterns are different in other languages, and your Spanish speakers or others can explain how.)

Before proceeding to the next pattern, it is very helpful for students to know the verbs that are always in the predicate and the coordinate conjunctions. Eventually, they should memorize these, but at first, they can refer to "A Summary of the Most Important Points for Memorization."

T: Now, change the verb from action to linking. If a verb "links" a subject to the rest of the sentence, it is a linking verb.

The pitcher is a star.

T: What is the action or link?

C: *Is;* therefore, *is* is the verb.

T: There is no action. *Is* is linking the subject to its complement and is called the linking verb.

T: Who or what is a star?

C: The *pitcher;* therefore, *pitcher* is the subject.

T: What is the pattern so far?

C: S+V

T: What is the question:

C: The pitcher is what?

T: What is the answer that completes the pattern?

C: Star.

T: What does the word star do in the sentence?

C: *Star* follows a linking verb and renames the subject; therefore, *star* is a predicate noun.

T: What is the pattern?

C: S+V+PN.

S + V + PN

The pitcher is a star.

T: If you change the part of speech of *star* from the noun to an adjective *fantastic* and put it in the same slot, you have, "The pitcher is fantastic." Analyze this one.

The pitcher is fantastic.

C: The action or link is *is;* therefore, *is* is the verb, a linking verb. Who or what is a star? The *pitcher*; therefore, *pitcher* is the subject. The pitcher is what? *Fantastic*; therefore, *fantastic* is the predicate adjective because it follows a linking verb and describes the subject.

S + V + PA

The pitcher is fantastic.

Obviously, you will practice many examples for each pattern before moving to the next, and the class does not respond this quickly, nor is Sam's friend actually in the class, but you get the idea. Teach the process. Note the flow chart in the appendix to chart the thinking process in this method of study. (Appendix III)

Having introduced the patterns, you now teach the parts of speech. Many grammar texts introduce the parts of speech first, and unfortunately, following this method is possibly why teaching syntax fails. The parts of speech vary according to their use and placement in a sentence, and therefore, are not helpful in understanding a pattern. Consider the word *light*.

Light my fire.
The *light* is bright.
He wore a *light* coat.

And what part of speech is *light*? It is a verb, noun, and adjective respectively. Do the pattern first. Make certain the class is comfortable with very simple examples that only contain the specific sentence parts in the basic five patterns, and then move to Parts of Speech.

T: Class, analyze, "Light my fire."

C: The action is *light*; therefore, *light* is the verb. Who or what lights?

(Depending on their training, they may have no response. This sentence is a command with the understood subject *you*.) You light what? *Fire*; therefore, *fire* is the direct object because *fire* receives the action of being lit.

S + V + DO
(you) Light my fire.

T: Once the pattern is completed, analyze the parts of speech. What is *light* doing in the sentence? Showing action; therefore, *light* is a verb. What is *fire* doing in the sentence? Naming; therefore, *fire* is a noun.

After labeling the parts of speech of the sentence parts, you should ask yourself, "What is left?"

My is left. What is *my* doing in the sentence? It is affecting the noun *fire*. What affects or modifies a noun? An adjective; therefore, *my* is an adjective. (Seeing *my* as a possessive pronoun has nothing to do with analyzing sentence structure so save this response for later.)

The steps are always the same. After labeling the sentence pattern, the questions is, "What's left?" Single words will be conjunctions, adjectives and adverbs. Prepositions will be a part of a phrase which is covered shortly under Phrases.)

(you) Light my fire.
      v   adj   n

C: In the second example, the linking verb is *is*. What is bright? The *light*; therefore, *light* is the subject. The light is what? *Bright*; therefore, *bright* is the predicate adjective because it follows a linking verb and describes the subject. In this example, *light* is a noun because it is the name, and *fire* is a noun because it is also a name. As always, the predicate is a verb. This example shows the change in the part of speech of *light* from a verb to a noun.

S + V + PA
The light is bright.
　　n　　v　adj

In the last example, *wore* is the action verb. Who wore the light coat? *He* did. Therefore, *he* is the subject. He wore what? A *coat*; therefore, *coat* is the direct object because it receives the action of being worn. What's left? *Light.* What is *light* doing in the sentence? It is modifying (describing, affecting) the noun *coat.* What affects a noun? An adjective; therefore, *light* is an adjective.

S + V + DO
He wore a light coat.
pro　v　　adj　n

(Explain that pronouns are more thoroughly covered in the next unit on usage. Do a few sentences with coordinate conjunctions and adverbs. Have students create sentences using all of the parts of speech such as "He wore a hat and a very light coat to the store." It is difficult for a teacher to accept that little practice is needed on parts of speech, but the point is just that. Parts of Speech are not what matter. The Parts of a Sentence in the pattern are the focus.)

To reiterate, a word's part of speech changes according to the job the word does in the sentence pattern. The sentence pattern must be taught first, and then the part of speech. Students have to always identify the sentence pattern before considering the parts of speech of each individual word. Text books usually begin with parts of speech, and many teachers follow the book, and confusion results. And, another problem with following a textbook is that once the very simple sentence is covered, the sentences suddenly shift and become far too complicated and contain too many unknowns. To return to the original jigsaw puzzle analogy, too many puzzle pieces still need to be covered so the examples have to remain controlled and simple. And still another reason that "grammar" instruction doesn't work is that teachers only cover parts of speech and some patterns. Who can solve a puzzle with missing pieces? The entire chart has to be covered to be effective. It seems a lot for a student to handle, but having the whole puzzle is why this method works as opposed to a piece here and a piece two grade levels later. Do children learn only part of language at a time? They get all of it all the time all at once, and their marvelous brains sort it out. Trust their brains and time to practice to do the same with analyzing what they do so naturally.

It is not necessary to label the articles, *a*, *an*, and *the*. Sometimes these three words are referred to as articles, sometimes adjectives. They are always the same and not a sentence part in the pattern so it unnecessary to label them and clutter the markings of the pattern. The best way to describe *a*, *an*, and *the* is as determiners because they determine or signal the reader that a noun is coming up in the pattern. In a discussion of the articles, it is interesting to compare English articles to French and Spanish.

INTRODUCING PHRASES

After practicing marking very simple examples of the basic sentence patterns and parts of speech, students are ready for Part III of the Chart:

Review the terms and definitions.

III. Phrase: a group of words
    A. Prepositional: prep + noun or pronoun
    B. Verbal: verbs acting like other parts of speech, n., adj., adv.
        1. participle: acts like an adj (many endings)
        2. infinitive: to + verb, acts like a n., adj., adv.
        3. gerund: ends in *ing* and acts like a n.

Follow the chart. After labeling the sentence pattern, students ask, "What's left?" What is left will be single words that are conjunctions or modifiers or phrases.

There are two types of phrases: prepositional and verbal.

By definition, a prepositional phrase begins with a preposition and ends with a noun or pronoun. Students will put a line through the prepositional phrase beginning with the preposition and ending with the noun. It should be a single line, not an *X*.

After students label a pattern, they go back and label the parts of speech of the pattern parts. They are developing the concept of slots in a pattern where certain parts of speech fit. Diagramming sentences illustrates this concept very well for students as long as the teacher and/or students do not get more concerned about correct and neat diagrams in place of understanding patterns and slots for parts of speech.

The pattern or kernel is on the base line of a diagram.

S	V	DO		S	V	PA
n	v	n		n	v	adj

The vertical line cuts the base line between the subject and the predicate, and the vertical line between the complements, the direct object and predicate complements, is perpendicular to the base line or slants respectively. The modifiers are below the base beneath the words they modify.

In labeling the sentences, rather than diagramming, the sentence word order or syntax is not distorted, and the importance of the pattern is emphasized with the sentence parts on top. The emphasis of the parts of speech is to see that nouns and pronouns fill subject, predicate noun, and all object slots. Single words or phrases are "what's left."

The very colorful parrot adeptly tossed me the cracker.

		S	+	V + IO	DO
very	colorful	parrot	adeptly	tossed me	cracker
adv	adj	**N**	adv	**PRO**	**N**

(I use modifies, describes, and affects interchangeably. *Modifies* is the correct term and must be used but requires a definition. *Describes* is the least desirable term, but the one students like. *Affects* is easy to understand and not so exacting as describes suggests.)

T: What's left?
C: *Very, colorful, adeptly*
T: What does *colorful* do in the sentence?
C: It affects the noun *parrot*.
T: What affects a noun?
C: An adjective; therefore, *colorful* is an adjective.
T: What else?
C: *Very* which affects *colorful*. Adverbs affect adjectives; therefore, *very* is an adverb.
T: Next?
C: *Adeptly* affects the verb *tossed*. Adverbs affect verbs; therefore, *adeptly* is an adverb.

Do not include prepositional phrases in the sentence practice until students can identify the conjunctions and modifiers. (Remember you always go through all of the steps to reinforce what students already know.)

We sat silently in the park until dusk.

C: The verb is sat. Who sat? We. The pattern is S + V. What's left? **A group of words,** *in the park* **go together and** *until dusk.* **A group of words is a phrase;** *in* **and** *until* **are not verbs but prepositions; therefore,** *in the pa*rk **and** *until dusk* **are prepositional phrases.**
Prepositional phrases are very easy to understand, and may already be in place. The real objective is to distinguish prepositional phrases from verbals. For example, *to the park* is not the same as *to park*. Students can think of prepositions as the relationship of the squirrel to the tree: *up* the tree, *down* the tree, *around* the tree, *through* the tree, etc. When students complete prepositional phrases, they are ready for verbals. Verbals are the heart of mature writing.

A verbal is first of all a verb, BUT, it does not do verb work. It does not show action nor link the subject with its complement (direct object or predicate noun or pronoun). Instead, this verb, the verbal, acts like a noun, an adjective, or an adverb doing naming or modifying work rather than predicate work. There are three types of verbals, and they can be single words or occur in phrases.

Again, be certain to use very simple examples.

On the board write four sentences. These verbals are labeled with specific markings, which unfortunately, this format does not permit illustrating. However, students need to mark these structures differently than others to better see how they function. They will put an X on single participles or across entire participial phrases, parentheses around an infinitive or entire infinitive phrases, and circles around gerunds and entire gerund phrases. **Remember that each of these verbals functions as different parts of speech, and the task is to comprehend that entire phrases are single parts of speech doing modifying and naming work instead of action.**

V

1.) The bird is singing.
2.) The singing bird is happy. (*Singing* would have an X on it.)
3.) The bird likes (to sing).
4.) Singing is fun. (When labeled, singing would have a circle around it, but this format does not permit that illustration.)

Ask the class in which sentence is a form of *sing* the predicate? Label the pattern in the first sentence. What is the action? Singing. Who or what is singing? The bird; therefore, the pattern is S +V. *Is singing* in the first sentence is a predicate because *singing* shows the action. *Is* is the helping verb. Remember that four verbs may comprise a predicate.

Identify the pattern in the second sentence. What is the verb? Is (a linking verb). Who is happy? The bird; therefore, *bird* is the subject. The bird is what? Happy; therefore, *happy* is the predicate adjective because it follows a linking verb and describes the subject. The pattern is complete: S + V + PA.

What's left? Singing. What is *singing* doing in the sentence? It is describing the noun bird. It is telling which bird, but *singing* is a verb. What is a verb acting like an adjective? A participle. Sentence #2 is the example of a participle. Place and X over the word *singing*.

Identify the pattern in the third sentence. What is the verb? Likes (an action verb). Who or what likes to sing? The bird; therefore, bird is the subject. The bird likes what? Here, the student makes a giant leap. The bird does not like *sing*. The bird does not like *to*. The entire phrase (*to sing*) is required to express the **IDEA**. Remember learning that a noun is a person, place, or idea? This infinitive (*to sing*) names the idea, acts like a noun, and fills the noun slot. **(TO SING) IS THE DIRECT OBJECT. STUDENTS MUST NOW SEE THAT A PHRASE (AND LATER A CLAUSE) CAN FUNCTION AS A NOUN. NOUNS ARE NOT ALWAYS SINGLE WORDS. THE CONCEPT IS DEEPER THAN THAT.** (For top students, comparing verbal phrases to quantities in algebra helps them to grasp the idea.) It is this idea of a noun that is not grasped by many teachers who must teach such concepts. Place parentheses around the infinitive phrase *to sing*.

Identify the pattern in the fourth sentence. What is the verb? Is (linking). Who or what is fun? Singing. Wait. *Singing* is a verb? How can a verb be a subject? *Singing* is the name of the activity that is fun. Verbs that end in *ing* and act like nouns are gerunds. Students know this definition. Therefore, the noun subject in this example is the gerund *singing*. Finish the pattern. Singing is what? Fun. Therefore, *fun* is the predicate adjective that follows the linking verb and describes the subject. Circle the gerund.

Show the class now that phrases gobble up, like little pac men, many ideas.

Singing in the shower in the morning begins my day.

What is the verb? Begins. What begins my day? Singing? Not just singing. The idea being expressed is not that *singing* begins the day but that singing in the *shower* in the morning begins the day. The gerund gobbles up the prepositional phrase, and the entire gerund phrase functions as the noun subject in the sentence. The entire phrase is circled.

INTRODUCING CLAUSES

It is important to remember the difference between a phrase and a clause. A phrase is a group of words that expresses a unit of thought. A clause is also a group of words but with a subject and verb (predicate). A clause contains one of the basic patterns. Review the following outline with the students, and once again refer to the flow chart.

IV. Clause-a group of words with a subject and a verb

    A. Independent clause-a clause that stands alone and expresses a complete thought

    B. Dependent clause-a clause that does not stand alone because it does not express a complete thought

        1. Noun clause-a dependent clause that acts like a noun

            a. relative pronouns introduce adjective and noun clauses

            b. examples: who whom, whose, which, that

        2. Adjective dependent clause-a dependent clause that acts like an adjective

        3. Adverb dependent clause-a dependent clause that acts like an adverb

            a. subordinate conjunctions introduce adverb clauses

            b. examples: as, if, since, when, after, because, unless, before, etc. (Do not memorize lists of these words because depending on the use in the sentence, many words like *since* and *before* can also be prepositions

To analyze the sentence for clauses, students ask the following questions:

Does the group of words have a pattern, a subject and a verb (predicate)?
    If yes, this group of words is a clause.
Does the clause express a complete idea and stand alone?
    If yes, the clause is independent. If no, the clause is dependent.
If the clause is dependent, what type of dependent clause is it? Does it act like a noun, adjective, or adverb? Knowing if the first word of the dependent clause is a subordinate conjunction or a relative pronoun helps identify the clause.

Students write adverbial dependent clauses developmentally much sooner than adjective and noun clauses so begin clause instruction with adverbial clauses.

When labeling dependent clauses, enclose them in brackets. Underline the independent clauses. Sometimes adverbial clauses are introductory and are set off with a comma, but if the adverbial clause is at the end of the independent clause, no comma is necessary. (Teach this punctuation rule as often as possible.)

[Before you cross the street], you should look both ways.
You should look both ways [before you cross the street].

Adjective clauses occur in the middle and end of sentences and begin with relative pronouns. Sometimes as with *that* the relative pronoun is omitted.

This room [that is always cold] is the library.
This room is the library [which is always cold].

The noun clause functions like a noun in the sentence and is therefore, a sentence part (S, DO, IO, PN). The noun clause can also be the noun object in a prepositional phrase.

$$S \quad + \quad V + PA$$
[That one must pay taxes] is certain.
$$\quad n \quad\quad\quad\quad\quad v \quad\quad adj$$

This structure, where the noun clause is a part of the sentence pattern is called embedding. What is the verb in the sentence? Is (linking). What is certain? *That one must pay taxes.* This clause, *that one must pay taxes,* a **noun** clause is the **name** of the subject or what is being talked about in the sentence. What is a noun? A noun is a syntactic structure that names. When students grasp embedding, a real comprehension of the structure of language is complete. Again, comparing embedding to quantities in algebra helps some students. They recognize and understand {[(. . .)]} this concept. Language works the same way.

S + V   +   DO
<u>Sam said [that he really learned a lot of syntax]</u>.
n   v   n

What is the verb? Said. Who said that he really learned a lot of syntax? Sam. Therefore, *Sam* is the subject. Sam said what? *That he really learned a lot of syntax.* Therefore, this dependent clause is the direct object in the pattern.

If you are just learning these concepts for the first time, you should be feeling more and more empowered by your understanding. You will be giving the same tool, a gift really, to your students soon.

Introducing Sentence Types

When students can mark the sentence patterns including prepositional and verbal phrases, they know how sentences in English are put together. English sentences are basically the patterns: S + V; S + V + DO; S + V + IO + DO; S + V +PN (PP); or S + V + PA. Within this basic pattern are phrases, prepositional and verbal, functioning as modifiers (adjectives or adverbs) and as sentence parts (subjects, direct objects, indirect objects and predicate nouns or pronouns, and predicate adjectives). These elements fit together to make the two kinds of clauses, independent or dependent, and finally, the kind of clause and number of them determine the type of sentence.

There are three sentence types: simple, compound, and complex. Review the definition of each.

A simple sentence is one independent clause.

A compound sentence is two or more independent clauses.

A complex sentence must have an independent clause plus at least one dependent clause. (The fourth type, compound complex, is just a combination but does not represent any new concepts.)

Another way to view sentence types is to see a simple sentence as one pattern. A compound sentence is two or more patterns. A complex sentence will have at least two patterns, but one of them will begin with a subordinate conjunction or a relative pronoun or will be dependent in some way on the independent pattern.

Children play. (simple)

Children play and laugh. (simple) There is a compound verb in this sentence, but there are not two patterns, so the sentence is still simple.

Children play, and they laugh. (compound) Now there are two patterns or two independent clauses so the sentence is compound.

[When children play], <u>they laugh</u>. (complex) Now one of the patterns is dependent on the other. This sentence is complex because of the introductory dependent clause and the independent clause.

It is a good idea at this point to learn two very important punctuation rules. Much of the study of syntax has been to improve a student's comprehension of these two rules.

When writing a compound sentence joined by a coordinate conjunction (and, or, but, nor, for, yet), use a comma in front of the coordinate conjunction.

<u>Children play</u>, and <u>they laugh</u>.

When writing a compound sentence without a coordinate conjunction, use a semi-colon.

<u>Children play</u>; <u>they laugh</u>.

When writing a complex sentence with an introductory adverbial dependent clause, use a comma.

[When children play], <u>they laugh</u>.

(Diagrammed sentences provide excellent visuals for sentence types!)

Also, now is the time to explain the sentence structural errors.

Anything punctuated as a sentence that does not contain an independent clause is a fragment. (Also explain that writing a fragment is not always an error, but one needs to know the rules to effectively break them. Most fragments are dependent clauses.) Omitting the comma or semi-colon is a run-on. Using a comma in place of the semi-colon is a comma splice. By always showing all three structures and errors together, students gain a better understanding of why they write fragments, run-ons, and comma splices. Because the structures look so similar, it is easy to confuse them.

Students have not fully mastered syntax until they can create their own structures. Level IV of the Chart is to be able to give examples of all of the structures. Notice that text books and worksheets are not necessary. Within a classroom are twenty or more creators of infinite variety and interest. When students are able to give examples of each of these structures, then they have a cool tool for analyzing their own writing and the writing of others. They now share a vocabulary with the teacher for writing conferences. Teachers have a short hand method for marking work. Revision for sentence variety will now make sense that goes beyond exercises in sentence combining or imitating the teacher's style. Comparison of other works helps a student analyze his/her own style as unique. Finally, though possibly not as exciting, students will be able to master the rest of all those errors: usage and mechanics.

Introduction to Usage

After teaching the syntax unit, the task is to apply this knowledge to usage problems. Show students how they are progressing up Bloom's Taxonomy from comprehending syntax to applying it to a problem in sentence structure. You are also concurrently re-teaching and/or reviewing, which reinforces the earlier instruction. This review process is why it is not necessary to insist on mastery too early. Now students will better understand usage problems. They will more easily edit their work and most importantly, retain the skill to do so.

Usage problems can be chunked into four major concerns: pronoun errors, subject-verb agreement errors, verb errors, and modifying errors. Pronoun errors are the most difficult to address because of the amount of new information. Subject-verb agreement, verbs, and modifiers follow. Covering pronouns first also allows more time and opportunity for review during the year.

It is important that the student understand your plan for their mastery of the concepts. It gives them a sense of security and consistency as you follow the same steps. Explaining the overall task also helps them to see that an end is in sight. The steps are learn the rule, learn the mistakes, practice, and then create correct and incorrect examples of the problem. Notice it is the same procedure as the vocabulary task. I do not know the problem, I know the problem, I can identify the problem, and finally, I can create correct and incorrect examples of the problem. Ultimately, the student is in control.

I have observed, and most of my students have agreed, that they work in a text book. The procedure is to read the rules, look at examples, do the exercises, correct errors, and then take a test. This is not real learning. This type of instruction will deliver a bell curve result, which the exercises are designed to do, and the status quo is maintained. Stronger, motivated students will make some progress, but not as much as is possible. The first step for the teacher is to pretest the students using tests that he/she designed which test only what addresses the errors. Share the pretest with the students and do a bell curve on the board. When you posttest, do the bell curve again. They see what learning actually is, and if the results are not high enough, reteach, and they know exactly what they have to do.

Some problems with testing are that high scoring students think they know everything. Low scoring students think they are stupid. Only addressing the errors and doing the bell curve levels the field, encouraging top students to actually study and improve and showing weaker students that these tests are only a question of learning rules. Tests are not measures of intelligence.

THE PROBLEMS WITH PRONOUNS

There are three errors that occur with pronouns. Use the mnemonic CAR to cue the students about the possibilities. CAR means case, agreement, and reference. Introduce each problem in the opposite order, however, from easy to more difficult.

The first challenge with correcting pronouns is obvious but overlooked. Students cannot fix what they cannot find. They have to be able to identify pronouns in a sentence. Teach the pronouns. (Again, pronoun usage is the most difficult problem; the other problems will be much easier.) There are five types of pronouns they need to recognize. There are others, but unless working with English language learners, the others are of minor concern. Students must memorize the five types: relative, interrogative, demonstrative, indefinite, and personal.

Relative pronouns: who, whom, whose, which, and that. These pronouns introduce noun and adjective clauses. However, students should already know these from the syntax unit so this is only review.

Interrogative pronouns: who, whom, whose, which, and what. These pronouns introduce questions. They only have to change *that* for *what* and these are learned. At this time illustrate the difference between a relative pronoun in a sentence and an interrogative pronoun.

I have students *who* love syntax.
Who loves syntax?

The relative pronoun introduces the dependent clause [*who loves syntax*], and the interrogative pronoun introduces the question.

Demonstrative pronouns: this, that, these, those. These pronouns point out things as near and far away. Here is another good opportunity to mention that when students are learning a foreign language, they need to memorize these words. They already know the words in English; they are just learning what to call them. Knowing how these words function ahead of time is very beneficial in learning a new language; otherwise, they have to do double duty.

Often, people say that they learned English grammar because they studied a second language. Knowing how languages work is extremely beneficial.

Give another example of how parts of speech differ according to their job in the sentence. Discuss the difference between *this* as a pronoun which replaces a noun and *this* as an adjective which affects a noun. (You have already taught this material; you are now reviewing and reinforcing.)

This is good.
This book is good.

Now is the time to also teach the reference error. In the sentence, "This is good," it is unclear what *this* means. This book? This story? This person? The error is called an indefinite reference because the antecedent (the noun the pronoun replaces) is unclear. Students usually make this mistake when they begin a sentence with the words *it* or *this*. In the second sentence, *this* is an adjective affecting the noun *book*. There is no pronoun because the noun *book* is given.

Indefinite pronouns: These pronouns are just that, indefinite as to a particular thing or person. They pose their own problem with number. Define number as a term meaning singular or plural. Indefinite pronouns can be singular, plural, or both.

Put a chart of indefinite pronouns on the wall and keep it there. You are after recognition here. Any grammar book has them, but you are teaching that someone, somebody, anyone, anybody, no one, nobody, etc. are singular. **The ones to pay attention to especially are everyone, everybody, each, either, and neither. They are singular.** Tests are designed with these latter pronouns because students make more mistakes with them than others.

Neither of the boys (like, likes) school.

Which verb is correct? Most students choose *like* because it sounds better. However, *likes* is correct because *neither* is the subject and it is singular. (The problem with indefinite pronouns is clearer when students work with subject-verb agreement errors.) Were you right? Sentences like this one are what are tested.

Plural pronouns like *many, both*, and *several* are not problems.

Indefinite pronouns like *some* really are not problems either but review the definition that a pronoun takes the place of a noun. The noun is the antecedent. Give two sentences:

Some is good.
Some are good.

Which sentence is correct? Both could be. It depends on the antecedent. Some salt is good; some people are good. In the first sentence *some* is singular because *salt* is singular. In the second sentence *some* is plural because *people* is plural.

Four of the five types are covered. (Now the real evil cometh. By now students may be freaking; just keep telling them the end is in sight.)

THE PROBLEM WITH
PERSONAL PRONOUNS

Begin the task of learning about personal pronouns by telling the students that personal pronouns are wicked. The students must not tell their parents that they are going to study them. Make them promise because it is necessary to be a bit wicked themselves to deal with the little devils.

Our first wicked deed is to do a little swearing. Just a little. Ask permission to do just a little. All smiles, they can't wait.

What you are doing is introducing the personal pronoun chart which they will have to, yes, you guessed it, memorize. Remember that when something is learned it is actually in memory. To move the knowledge from short term to long term memory, the learner memorized the information. The students will be able to edit a paper because they have memorized some rules. To empower themselves, they have to study.

T: Write the Personal Pronoun Chart on the board and then chant the terms in order:

I	we
you	you
he, she, it	they

I, you, he, she, it, we, you, they. Say it over and over and faster and faster. After the laugh, erase the board, face the class, and point in the air. Have the class call out the pronouns as you point up, down, left, right, etc. (Someone will ask why *you* is said twice which leads an explanation about number. *Number* means singular or plural. In English the same word *you* designates singular and plural, but other languages use different words. An added benefit of memorizing the pronoun chart is for students studying foreign language. They will be ahead of the game here, or you will be putting them ahead in their foreign language class.)

Put the Personal Pronoun Chart back on the board, and now label each part as you explain it. Label Singular and Plural. Then explain and label Person. Person indicates who is speaking. First person is the speaker: *I.* Second person is spoken to: *you.* Third person is spoken about: *he, she, it.*

Continue explaining to the class that they can see now why personal pronouns are so wicked because they have person and number. And what's worse, they have sex.

The sleeping members of the class are now awakened.

Well, what can we say? Personal pronouns have . . . and explain gender. Personal pronouns are masculine, feminine, or neuter. (Prepare for the class response.) Because students can tell that little boys are "he" and little girls are "she" and desks are "it," errors in gender are just careless mistakes and do not pose a problem.(Take this opportunity to point out that gender is a huge problem if they are learning languages like French or Spanish.) Pronouns seem complicated to students, but if you hold their interest, they do master them.

Now introduce the rule. Explain that the way to master pronoun usage and to improve test scores is to follow the same editing steps: know the rule, find the pronouns, apply the rule, and make the correct choice. If they follow the steps, they will not error.

In learning the rule, write the rule on the board, but write it **incorrectly**.

A pronoun agrees with their antecedent in person, number, and gender. Their case is determined by the sentence part.

Ask the class that, in fact, if, IF, they were ever taught anything about pronouns, if instruction followed this pattern: "Open your books to page such and such, someone read the rule, look over the examples, do the exercises, correct the one or two missed, take a test, and move on." I ask my students if they remained clueless? I have never had a student disagree.

Explain why they are having trouble. The aforementioned method just does not work. How could they correct a pronoun problem, if, in fact, they do not know what a pronoun is in the first place? Pointing to the rule, what does antecedent mean? What does agreement mean?

At this point take the entire rule apart teaching the vocabulary. They know what a *pronoun* is. It takes the place of a noun. In this particular case, these pronouns take the place of nouns referring to people or things. The *antecedent* is the noun the pronoun replaces. Give examples such as, "*I* put the *pen* on the desk. *I* put *it* on the desk. *It* is the pronoun, and *pen* is the antecedent. *I* is the pronoun: the *speaker* is the antecedent." "*Agreement* means the same. Now restate the rule in terms they understand. A pronoun, a word that replaces a noun, must be the same in person, number, and gender with the noun it replaces. When they agree that they know all of the terms, have them now apply the rule. Look at the sentence. (Remember that you wrote it incorrectly on the board because your pronoun and antecedent do not agree.) Tell the class they are on their first scavenger hunt, looking for a pronoun agreement problem. Follow the steps by first finding the pronoun. The pronoun in the rule is *their*. Now find the antecedent. The antecedent is *pronoun*. The words *pronoun* and *their* have to agree or be the same in person. They are both third person. (Remember they memorized the chart.) *Pronoun* and *their* have to agree or be the same in number. Ah, ha, they have found it. *Pronoun* is singular, but *their* is plural. They have found the agreement error and have an example of what the problem is, and now they must correct the sentence. They change the pronoun and call up from their memory what the third person singular pronoun is. Change all of the *their's* to *it*. Emphasize that most agreement problems are problems with number.

Now that the rule is corrected, the students must memorize it. Drill, drill, drill. Create a rhythm and recite the rule out loud with the class. Practice it all year. You could be taking attendance while they chant the rule.

When the first part of the rule is memorized, say, "Guess what? Pronouns are really, really wicked because we have only done the first half." (Groan. Teaching is work. Learning is harder work. Get over it, and move on to the second part of the pronoun problem.)

Its case is determined by the sentence part.

Explain case. Pronouns not only have person, number, and gender, but also case. Case means the form or way that the pronoun is written. The form of the pronoun, or the case, changes according to how it is used in the sentence. In other words, the sentence part determines the case. Ask the class if they have been corrected for saying, "Susie and me went to the show." The correct expression is, "Susie and I went to the show." Why? Sometimes, "Susie and me" is correct. "Please sit between Susie and me at the show." What changed? The part the pronoun played in the sentence changed, so the form or case of the pronoun had to change.

These two pronoun problems, agreement and case, are always on achievement tests. If you want students to score high, they have to understand these two problems. Understanding case is not easy, but you will enjoy, as the students do, when the light bulb clicks. Understanding, by the way, is not applying little "tricks." Teachers have students say the sentence without the first noun or pronoun. In a sentence such as, "Send the flowers to Susie and I, you would not say, 'Send the flowers to I.'" This method works for some students, but it is not really achieving an understanding of the concept of how the language is working, and tests are designed to identify real understanding. The test will say, "The students are they." That sentence is correct, but not one student in the class will mark it as such. Are these sentences correct? The students were he and she. It is I. The argument was between him and her. Which ones are correct? Which aren't? Are you 100% certain? They are all correct, and your students need to know exactly why to have the confidence to know they are right. Don't we all hate the part of the test that says, "All of the above"? Reiterate that they are becoming excellent game players in the scavenger hunt.

Pronouns have three cases: Nominative, Objective, and Possessive. Finish labeling the chart now. It is complete. Continue discussing the meanings of the words in the rule. Case (which you have now explained) is determined by the sentence part. They already know the sentence parts: subject, verb, direct object, indirect object, predicate noun, and predicate adjective. Since we are concerned with pronouns, verbs and predicate adjectives do not apply. Also explain that in the prepositional phrase, the noun or pronoun, is called the object. Pronouns can be used in the same positions in the sentence pattern as nouns: subject, predicate noun (but are called predicate pronouns), direct object, indirect object, and object of a preposition. (S, PP, DO, IO, OP) They have to memorize the nominative case pronouns. Oh wait, they already know them. Have them repeat, "I, you, he, she, it, we, you, they." The new information is that these pronouns are nominative case and are used as subjects and predicate pronouns in the sentence pattern. The objective case pronouns are used as direct objects, indirect objects and objects of prepositions in the sentence pattern. What are the objective case pronouns? They can figure them out easily since they know the nominative case forms. Write the second part of the chart with them. I have a book. Give the book to *me*. You have a book. Give the book to *you*. He has a book. Give the book to *him*, etc. Do Possessive Case at this point also. I have a book. It is *my* book. You have a book. It is *your* book. He has a book. It is *his* book, etc.

To finish the work with pronoun case, you must now put examples of the five sentence patterns on the board.

1. Susie and me have some tickets.
2. The players are Susie and me.
3. The coach called Susie and me.
4. The coach gave Susie and me some tickets.
5. The coach gave the tickets to Susie and me.

You could make all the pronouns nominative case or mix them up, but the idea is to show the pronoun in all five positions. The first two sentences are incorrect, and the last three are correct. Do not allow the students to go by sound. Remember that the tests are designed to account for that. Teach the students to follow the steps:

Find the pronoun.

Determine the sentence part.

Choose the correct case: subjects and predicate pronouns are nominative case, and all objects are objective case.

Choose the pronoun

In the first sentence, the pronoun is *me*. The verb is *have*. Who have the tickets? Susie and me. Therefore, *me* is the subject. Subjects require nominative case. Nominative case is *I*. *Me* is incorrect.

In the second sentence, the pronoun is *me*. The verb is *are*. *Are* is a linking verb; therefore, the pattern is S + V + PP. *Me* is a predicate pronoun. Predicate pronouns are nominative case. *Me* is objective case; therefore, *me* is incorrect. This sentence pattern is the one on ACT or SAT placement tests because it is the most often missed. *I* is nominative case and the correct pronoun.

In the third sentence, the pronoun is *me*. The verb is *called*. Who called Susie and me? The coach. *Coach* is the subject. The coach called whom? Susie and me. *Susie and me* are direct objects. Objects require objective case. *Me* is objective. Me is correct.

In the fourth sentence, the pronoun is *me*. The verb is *gave*. Who gave Susie and me the tickets? The coach. *Coach* is the subject. The coach gave what? Tickets. *Tickets* is the direct object. Who got the tickets or in other words, received the direct object? Susie and me. *Me* is an indirect object. Objects require objective case; therefore, *me* is correct because it is objective case.

In the fifth sentence, students really should be able to see the prepositional phrase. They should be proficient enough at this stage of instruction to just pick out prepositional phrases without any difficulty. Still, it does not hurt to practice. *Gave* is the verb. Who gave the tickets to Susie and me. Coach. *Coach* is the subject. The coach gave what? Tickets. *Tickets* is the direct object. The pattern is finished. What's left? The group of words *to Susie and me*. This is a phrase, one of two possibilities. Prepositional or verbal. There is no verb so this is not an infinitive. To + noun or pronoun. *Me* is the object of the preposition *to*. Objects are objective case; therefore, since *me* is objective, it is correct. Reading this makes the process seem dragged out and cumbersome, but remember that once the process is learned, it becomes automatic and the thinking is done in an instant—with confidence and without error. (Top students need to be convinced to follow the method. Because they are naturally proficient and already score well on tests, they are reluctant to question what they think is correct. However, the better they are the harder it is to define the one or two sentences that will stump them. Following the steps is the only guarantee.)

Of course, once you have spent real time on understanding the rule, students need to practice. Make certain, however, that the practice follows the design and that the lessons only cover the problems. Avoid practicing what they already know or introducing new information.

Hallelujah! The pronouns are fixed. Celebrate. Have a party. Maybe offer a party celebration before you begin pronouns because they are work. Now students can add pronouns to their ever growing scavenger list. Remember to practice reciting the rule often. Incorporating song or some rhythm to the recitation makes it stick in the students' memories. A PRO-noun a-GREES with its AN-te-CE-dent in PER-son, NUM-ber, and GEN-der. Its CASE is de-TER-mined by the SEN-tence PART.

One additional point for consideration is spelling. If students see the difference between objective and possessive case, then spelling you, your, yours, its, it's, their, theirs, they're makes sense. Possessive case pronouns do not have apostrophes, and these words always occur on placement tests. Contractions do use apostrophes that indicate the missing letters. Very good students need to be made aware that these little words are often read over and therefore, missed on tests.

The Problem of
Subject-Verb Agreement

If you did not teach the pronoun chart and the meaning of the term *number*, then you must do that now. (p. 72)

Students understand singular and plural as these terms apply to nouns. Begin by showing them that they can count the desks in the room. They understand that one desk is singular and two desks are plural. They know to add an *s* or *es* to make a singular noun plural.

With subject-verb agreement problems, students must learn that verbs have number. Thinking of verbs as singular or plural is sometimes difficult because they can count desks; they are tangible. A verb is not. Do they have one *is* or two? A verb cannot be counted like a desk. Students must learn that adding an *s* to a verb makes a verb singular. Unfortunately, it's the exact opposite of a noun. An *s* on a noun makes it plural, but an *s* on a verb makes it singular.

Write some verbs on the board. Jump. Singular or plural? Plural. Jumps? Singular. Write a mixed list of verbs on the board and have the students sort them by singular or plural. However you do it, make certain students realize that adding an *s* makes a verb singular.

Now they must learn the rule to add to the scavenger list. They need to know that subjects and verbs agree in number; both are singular or both are plural. Then they memorize the following rule:

A singular subject takes a singular verb, and singular verbs end in *s*.

It is not necessary to learn all aspects of this rule. If they know this part, the rest falls into place. They know that plural subjects then take plural verbs.

Explain to the students how smart they are. The reason they make mistakes or errors is BECAUSE they are smart. Learning a language is all about learning patterns. Because they are smart, they learn patterns very well. Unfortunately, the patterns sometimes change, and that's when the errors occur. Show them that 99% of all the sentences they write or say do not contain a subject-verb agreement error, but placement tests are looking for that student who knows the 1%. Their task is to identify where the pattern changes. They are on a scavenger hunt for the exceptions. There are only three of them. What you are doing now as the teacher is chunking the errors for recognition.

Show them that they already know to say, "I think, you think, he think**s**. I like, you like, he like**s**." They already automatically put that *s* ending on the third person singular when necessary. Show them then where the pattern is different. Write the following sentences on the board:

1. The student (like, likes) school.
2. One of the students (like, likes) school.
3. Neither of the students (like, likes) school.
4. The boy nor the girls (like, likes) school.
5. The girls nor the boy (like, likes) school.

Have the students cross out (always cross out) the incorrect verbs so the sentence reads correctly.

Students must learn to follow specific steps for editing usage problems. (1) Analyze the sentence for the subject and verb. Of course, in these examples the verb is given, but in real writing or testing, they have to be able to find the verb. Once again, an understanding of syntax is essential. How does one correct a subject and verb agreement problem if one cannot find the subject and verb?

In Sentence #1, the verb is *like* or *likes*. Who likes school? The boy. Therefore, *boy* is the subject. (Always go through the steps for analyzing the sentence structure for review and retention.)

(2)Next determine the number of the subject. The subject determines what the number of the verb must be. *Boy* is the singular subject.

(3)Now apply the rule. A singular subject like boy takes a singular verb that ends in *s*. Therefore, *likes* is correct.

Sentence #2 illustrates the way tests are designed to elicit student errors because Sentence #2 contains a prepositional phrase. (Syntax again.) Always emphasize the test design for the student so they have the edge on "winning the game" or scoring high. In patterns like Sentence #2, students must cross out all of the prepositional phrases. The subject of a sentence is NOT in the prepositional phrase. This agreement problem is why you have had the students cross out the prepositional phrases when they were learning syntax. More and more now the foundation of the syntax study will become apparent and useful. You are now connecting a tool to its application and moving up Bloom's Taxonomy. The subject of Sentence #2 is *One,* not *boys. One* is singular; therefore, the verb is singular and ends in *s. Likes* is correct.

Sentence #3 is the sentence that identifies the verbally gifted students on a placement test. Sentence #3 illustrates the problem with indefinite pronouns. Their number is as the name indicates. Some are singular, some are plural, and some are both. Having already learned these pronouns, students are ready to apply this knowledge. In Sentence #3, the subject is *Neither.* If you use this sentence as a pretest, most students will miss it because they read *boys* and focus on the stronger noun rather than the pronoun, and *boys like* sounds better. If you want to raise scores, this pattern is the one to practice. Since *neither* is the indefinite singular pronoun and the subject of the sentence, the correct verb ends in *s* making *likes* the choice. Again, they cross out the prepositional phrase because the subject is not in a prepositional phrase.

Sentence #4 is also a pattern for the verbally talented. In this example, there are two subjects. The coordinate conjunction, however, is not AND. When the coordinate conjunctions are *or* or *nor,* they do not mean both subjects but one or the other. The verb does not agree with both subjects. The verb agrees with the subject that is closer to the verb. In a question it is the first subject; otherwise, it is the last subject. In the example, the subjects are *boy* and *girls. Girls* is closer to the verb; therefore, the plural subject *girls* takes the plural verb like, the verb that does not end in *s*.

In Sentence #5, the closer subject to the verb is *boy* and the singular verb *likes* is correct.

Editing or testing for subject-verb agreement errors is not about picking what sounds right, but knowing to look for this error and then to follow the steps to correct if necessary. Remember, the writer or test taker must know when he/she is correct also.

In working with subject-verb agreement problems, teachers must spend this amount of explanation and pre-teaching before any worksheet practice will be effective. Also, the practice must focus only on the possible errors first grouped according to the patterns illustrated in #1-5, and then with mixed patterns. If you examine an exercise in a text, there are easy responses which students do not miss. Doing these is a waste of time. Do not work with what students already know or need not practice. Pretest, teach, posttest, reteach.

To summarize, practice the rule with rhythm until it is memorized. Memorize the three ways the language or the test designer "tricks" the students with 1.) prepositional phrases, 2.) indefinite pronouns, and 3.) with compound subjects joined by *or* or *nor*, the verb agrees with the closer subject.

The scavenger hunt list now includes pronoun errors, the CAR, case, agreement, and reference, and subject-verb agreement with its three possibilities to trick them. Now you move on to verb errors. It gets easier and easier.

THE PROBLEM WITH VERBS

In order to edit problems with this part of speech, the verb, a little background study is helpful.

English verbs can be written in four possible forms. These forms are called the principal parts of a verb. (Read carefully.) The four principal parts are the present participle principal part, the present principal part, the past principal part, and the past participle principal part. (Enough *p*'s for you?) The repetition, here, of the term principal part is intentional in order to emphasize that principal parts are names of forms of verbs, not names of tenses. Unfortunately, since the names of the tenses are similar, the two concepts get confused. Principal parts are the names of the ways to write a verb form.

Besides understanding the term principal parts, students need to learn that verbs are classified as regular or irregular depending on how they form their principal parts. A regular verb obviously forms its principal parts in a "regular" way, or in other words, regular verbs follow a consistent pattern like adding *ed* to the ending in the past and past participle principal parts. Tell students again that they error only because the pattern changes not because they lack intelligence. You cannot emphasize enough that they make mistakes BECAUSE their brains do what they are designed to do, not because they are not smart.

Study the chart.

Principal Parts

Present Participle	Present	Past	Past Participle
walking	(to) walk	walked	(have) walked
talking	(to) talk	talked	(have) talked
climbing	(to) climb	climbed	(have) climbed

These are regular verbs. Show students that the verbals are derived from these principal parts. The gerund and present participle are formed by adding *ing* to the present participle principal part. If the present participle principal part does naming or noun work in the sentence, it is called a gerund. If the present participle principal part does a modifying job in a sentence, it is called a participle. Participles can be both present and past. (The *breaking* glass startled us. The *broken* glass was dangerous.) The base form, or present principal part, becomes the infinitive when the word *to* precedes it as illustrated in the chart above.

Now consider the irregular classification of verbs. Irregular verbs form their principal parts in an irregular manner.

Present Participle	Present	Past	Past Participle
singing	(to) sing	sang	(have) sung
ringing	(to) ring	rang	(have) rung
bringing	(to) bring	brang	(have) brung
OOPS			

And here you reiterate that the students are smart. Their brains learn sing, sang, sung. Ring, rang, rung. Anyone with a functioning brain knows that logically it is bring, brang, brung, but not so in English. You have illustrated the error often tested: bring, brought, brought.

Having examined the underlying structure of the predicate (verb), it is time to identify the editing problem or errors to find.

One error to identify is using the wrong form or principal part of the verb and not knowing what the correct forms are. Now is the time for a dictionary lesson. No one can know all of the correct forms for the 200+ irregular verbs in English. However, take heart, they know almost all of them, and their education will teach the most commonly missed and tested ones. For all others, the dictionary will tell them the irregular forms for any irregular verb. Problem solved. Tell the class not to complain. Imagine learning to speak English as a second language and having to deal with over two hundred problems.

The second error is using the wrong principal part to form a tense. Give the example, "Today I *drink* milk. Yesterday I *drank* milk. Many times I *have drunk* milk. Today I *swim* in the lake. Yesterday I *swam* in the lake. Many times I *have swum* in the lake. Today I *run* a mile. Yesterday I *ran* a mile. Many times I *have run* a mile." Also include the infamous, "Today I *lie* on the couch. Yesterday I *lay* on the couch. Many times I *have lain* on the couch." Who says, "lain" anymore? But tests keep testing this particular verb so do not ignore it.

Now explain tense to the students. There is much more to tense and conjugation, but you are only concerned, remember, with where the errors are hidden. Conjugate a verb for the class. (Connect with foreign language instruction again also.)

The use of *shall* in first person is formal, standard English. It is information to note but not essential. Do point out the change in the pattern in third person singular to reteach the reason for the subject-verb agreement problem.

The principal parts form the tenses: sing, sang, sung

Present Tense	Past Tense	Future Tense
I sing	I sang	I shall sing
you sing	you sang	you will sing
he sings	he sang	he will sing
we sing	we sang	we shall sing
you sing	you sang	you will sing
they sing	they sang	they will sing

Present Perfect Tense	Past Perfect Tense	Future Perfect Tense
I have sung	I had sung	I shall have sung
you have sung	you had sung	you will have sung
he has sung	he had sung	he will have sung
we have sung	we had sung	we shall have sung
you have sung	you had sung	you will have sung
they have sung	they had sung	they will have sung

You are now ready to explain the most tested verb error. It is incorrect to use the past principal part like *sang* in a perfect tense. The perfect tenses have helping verbs and use the past participle principal part like *sung* not the past principal part *sang*. Give many examples, and by this time of year, you know your students and know the verbs they misuse the most. To say, "I *have ran*, I *have went*, I *have swam*, the bell *has rang*" is incorrect. These verbs are the past principal part form. They should be, "I *have run*, I *have gone*, I *have swum*, the bell *has rung*." The grammar text always covers the ones usually tested. Defining what a helping verb is works now. Verbs are called helping verbs (also called auxiliary but an unnecessary vocabulary lesson) because they "help" determine the number (singular like *has* or plural like *have*) and tense of the predicate/verb (present like *have* and past like *had*) in the sentence.

To summarize, students must understand what an irregular verb is and know the principal parts. They must then know to use the past participle form in the perfect tenses, the ones with a helping verb. Note that the present participle follows the pattern. Even the most irregular verb *to be* is regular in the present participle form, *being*. Adding *ing* to the base forms the present participle. Since there are no exceptions, there are no errors. Therefore, when drilling the principal parts of the irregular verbs, students only need to do the present, past, and past participle forms.

As students gain mastery of their editing skills, they begin to see how parts overlap and support one another and that there is a structure and logic to the rules. Textbooks are cluttered with too many problems in an effort to address all possibilities. Students are not going to say, "Scissors is." They use compound subjects without personal pronouns correctly. Most of their language skills are fine. Chunking the major errors and keeping the focus on errors alone, dramatically improves the student's performance. (Although there is much more to understanding tense, what students need has been covered.)

THE PROBLEM WITH MODIFIERS

The most difficult work is over. Modifiers are easy providing the student knows what a modifier is. (You have covered this.) Remind students that adjectives and adverbs are modifiers because they affect or change other parts of speech in a sentence. There are four modifying mistakes, but only three are tested. Misplaced modifiers are best taught as they occur in the students' writing. However, do cover all four modifying errors.

1.) Good and well. Adjectives and adverbs are often incorrectly interchanged. It is incorrect to say, "I did good on the test." Go back to syntax and analyze the sentence. Did is the verb. Who did good on the test? I. I is the subject. I did what? There is no answer. Good is in the direct object slot but is not being done. The pattern is S + V. What's left? *Good* and *on the test*. *On the test* is a group of words. There is no verb; therefore, *on the test* is a prepositional phrase beginning with the prep and ending with the noun. Know your students. If they understand syntax and do not need to practice the method, then they know immediately what the pattern is, and that *good* is affecting or modifying *did* because it is telling how something was done. Adverbs tell how. So *good* is functioning as an adverb. However, *good* is an adjective. The adverbial form of good is *well*. Hence, the error. The sentence should be, "I did well on the test." Then say, "I did real well on the test." The sentence is also incorrect because real is modifying well. (An adverb modifying another adverb. Remember the definitions.) The adverbial form of real is really. "I did really well on the test" is correct.

2.) Double negatives. "I don't never understand syntax." Do not use two negatives in the same sentence.

54

3.) Comparisons of adjectives and adverbs. This problem is the question used to separate the "best" student from the others. Create the awareness that the student's ability to say *taller* rather than *more taller* is tested. Never do both of the methods at the same time. If there are doubts as to how the comparisons are formed, the dictionary gives the irregular modifiers using more or most. Students do need to practice this, but the real question is that in the comparative taller (no need to learn the term comparative), the comparison is for TWO things. The superlative form is used for three or more. Students can count. It is not so much a matter of understanding how to fix the error but of creating an awareness that the problem exists.

Of the *three* hats I like the blue one best.
Of the *two* hats I like the blue one better.

Of all the boys Sam is the tallest.
Of the two boys Sam is the taller.

4.) Misplaced modifiers. The error is exactly what it says. Often it involves putting a participial phrase too far from the noun it is modifying or a prepositional phrase in the wrong place. The error is best taught as it occurs in the student's writing. There are many humorous examples on the internet of this error but read before using them in class.

And usage is done.

These problems are easy to understand and cover. The objective is to create an awareness of what is being tested and to add to the scavenger list. These are minor errors in the whole scheme of possible writing problems, but they are always tested. By now you should sense the unfairness of using a standardized test to determine one's acceptance to any learning situation.

To review: The scavenger hunt is now the SU of all those errors. The student now edits all writing/speaking according to sentence structure (fragments, run-ons, comma splices) and usage (pronouns, subject-verb agreement, verbs, and modifiers.)

A second purpose for my writing this book is to offer suggestions as to how a teacher achieves higher thinking skills. The expression, itself, is ambiguous or at least complex at best. However, consider that if a student now understands syntax, the two of you, student and teacher, have a common vocabulary and a tool that, together, you can apply to writing. Understanding language to improve one's speaking, writing, and ultimately, thinking is the real objective of a language arts class. Now difficult concepts such as parallelism make sense. Students can better revise their work, a higher level of thinking involving analysis and application of learned concepts as well as synthesis and evaluation as the student communicates.

Good writing requires a mature sentence length. (The length of the sentence is how a computer is evaluating a student's writing. Hemingway, of course, would fail.) Applying the content knowledge to their writing as the objective of studying syntax is on a much higher level of thinking than picking nouns out of a sentence on a worksheet which is how the effectiveness of syntax instruction is measured.

The only syntax instruction that shows a correlation to improved writing is sentence combining. What the student is actually doing is manipulating the various syntactic structures. However, the student is merely imitating and not really understanding. They are working with artificial sentences rather than their own style and level of ability. It is far more difficult to achieve this depth of understanding, but it is really what the study of language, the art of language, should be.

It is exciting to sit with a student and really analyze his/her writing. Also, group work is very productive now, because the students really understand editing and revision of sentence structure.

Now consider a group of students evaluating a sample of writing for clarity and conciseness. There are no absolutes now. Students can manipulate sentence structures and make evaluative decisions. Does the student want rapid fire, short sentences as Hemingway would use for a battle scene? Is it possible to be less wordy by using verbals? Telling students to be concise and clear is less ambiguous when specific reasons are given. Real comprehension by the students is far superior to imitating a text through sentence combining or relying on a teacher's revision.

MECHANICS (PUNCTUATION AND CAPITALIZATION)

The third and final part of SUM or basic skill instruction is the M for mechanics: punctuation and capitalization. Organize all of the rules for your students by chunking them into three categories: miscellaneous marks, the ubiquitous comma, and dialogue. Avoid the hit and miss approach of a worksheet one day on dialogue and another worksheet on another day about the comma. This method leaves the student with the task of organizing all of the knowledge. It's too hard to do.

Miscellaneous Marks. Ask students what punctuation marks there are. They will get most of them. Save the comma for its own lesson. Students should be able to name six miscellaneous marks. (Parentheses and brackets, etc. are not tested and really fall into much later writing experiences so skip them and tell students not to use them.) Group the six miscellaneous marks for easier recall. Remind students they are on a scavenger hunt for these and need to be consciously looking for them to correct them (or know if they are already correct). Editing is not a matter of the error jumping out at the writer which is what is happening in student group work. The younger, inexperienced writers think everything sounds fine, and they read their writing, *if* they reread it, the way they think they wrote it.

The six miscellaneous marks are colon, semi-colon, quotation marks, underlining (italics now possible with computers), hyphens, and apostrophes. Encourage students by explaining that it only takes two class periods to go over them, and they are set. Chunked together and presented as a whole, learning the marks does not seem like an endless, impossible task. You are after the feeling on the part of the student, "Is that all? And I'm done? I can do that!" Taking only two class periods to explain only the errors provides students with this sense of completion and possible success. Also, they already know more than they realize and will gain confidence when they do realize it.

Colon (:) The colon is used for time. (2:00 P.M.)

The greeting in a business letter. (Dear Sir:)

And the one on placement tests, items to follow. Explain that they already know two of the three. The problem is the last one, so by learning just this one error, they will score higher. Write the incorrect example, "I bought: milk, sugar, and bread." This sentence is incorrect because they must not separate the parts of the sentence pattern. Students will tell you that they punctate according to where the stops are. That method is not effective. Real rules based on syntactic structures always work. Back to syntax. Do not put a colon between a predicate (verb) and its direct object. Complete the pattern and then place the colon at the end of the pattern. I bought these items: milk, sugar, and bread. The word *items* is the direct object and is not separated from its verb. The pattern is complete: S+V+DO and then the list follows.

Semi-colon (;) There is only one use for the semi-colon that matters with regards to testing and student writing. A semi-colon is used to separate two independent clauses that do NOT have a coordinate conjunction. (Notice that the rule makes perfect sense because students know what a coordinate conjunction is and what an independent clause is.) To separate the two clauses with a comma is the infamous comma splice error. It is incorrect to "splice" together the two clauses with a tiny comma. The connection requires a semi-colon. To omit any mark is a run-on. Students now understand these two major structural errors, the CS and the Run-on, and can correct them.

In practicing the examples, use very simple sentences at first. A little drama or a lot is also effective. Some professionals argue that dramatics in the classroom are not necessary, but if you can do it, why not? Students engage and love it. These are serious structural errors that keep students out of credit classes in college and put them into remedial ones. Being a totally hysterical witch, costume and all, to eliminate the wicked elements of language arts is welcomed by students. Comic relief is a good thing. It is never too early nor too often to practice the exorcism of the comma splice.

Students must see the difference in structure of the following sentences:

I fell, and I cried. This is a compound sentence WITH a coordinate conjunction *and* requiring the comma. (Remember that the students have memorized and will sing the coordinate conjunctions for you: *and, or, but, nor, for,* and *yet*.

I fell; I cried. This is a compound sentence WITHOUT a coordinate conjunction requiring a semi-colon. There is no coordinate conjunction.

Note that the placement tests are designed to find the very good students. The test question will ask which of the following sentences is punctuated correctly.

1. I fell and I cried.
2. I fell; and I cried.
3. I fell, therefore, I cried.
4. None of the above.

Students hear the break and go for #3. *Therefore* interrupts the sentence, and interrupters are set off, but *therefore* is not a coordinate conjunction.

I fell**; therefore,** I cried.

The correct punctuation is the semi-colon between the two independent clauses. A comma follows *therefore* which is an introductory word in the second clause.

Quotation Marks and Underlining (" " ___)For some reason, and I blame everyone and everything, this is one difficult rule to learn and apply. It is incorrectly done by everyone and everything, especially T.V., texts, etc. One would wonder that since everyone ignores or does not know the rule, then why have it? When the rule stops appearing on placement tests, then we can abandon it as a measure of a student's ability. The rule is not difficult: Put quotation marks around short works like short stories, poems, parts of larger works like articles and chapters. Underline longer works like novels, plays, newspapers, magazines, and also art work, trains, planes (but not automobiles.) The CD title is underlined; each individual song would be in quotes. The title of a TV program is underlined; each episode is in quotes. Underlining is the same as italics, but do not use both. This is not a difficult rule, but students have trouble applying it.

Hyphen (-) Words are hyphenated between syllables, and hyphenated words interfere with reading fluency. Tell students to stop hyphening words, and the problem is solved.

Use the hyphen for written numbers twenty-one to ninety-nine.
The less familiar rule involves fractions.

I want two-thirds of the pie.
I want two thirds.

Which sentence is correct? It is a matter of syntax, of course. If the fraction is an adjective, it is hyphenated. If the fraction is a noun, it is not hyphenated. In both sentences, two thirds is a noun functioning as the direct object in the sentence. Therefore, the second sentence is correct.

The senator needs a two-thirds majority to win.

In this example, *two-thirds* is an adjective modifying majority and is hyphenated. The fraction is what's left; the direct object or noun is *majority*.

Apostrophe (') The apostrophe is the bane of most adults' punctuation. It is a frequently used mark and the most misunderstood. Teach this mark at the beginning of a class and only cover it. Students like hearing that this is the mark that adults hate.

By middle school, students understand singular and plural nouns. Begin making a chart with singular nouns. Then have the class fill in all of the plural forms of these nouns. Emphasize that except in special situations, apostrophes are not used to form plurals. A common punctuation mistake for students is to use the apostrophe for form plural nouns. (Apostrophes are used to form the plural of letters and words referred to as such: too many *and*'s or *e*'s. These words and letters are also in italics.)

Once the singular and plural nouns are on the chart, explain the three rules for apostrophes beginning with the singular form. Follow the steps.

For singular possessives, (1) **write the singular form** and add '_s_ Forget about the singular nouns ending in _s_. If '_s_ is added, it is still correct.

Put a chart on the board. Wait to fill in the plural possessive until you are discussing the second and third steps for placing the apostrophe.

Singular Nouns	Singular Possessives	Plural Nouns	Plural Possessive
dog	dog's bone	dogs	dogs' bones
girl	girl's bat	girls	girls' bats
man	man's hat	men	men's hats
child	child's tog	children	children's toys

Next do the plural possessive. Follow the steps.

(2) **Write the plural form.**

(3) **Look at the ending**. If it **ends in _s_**, put the apostrophe after the _s_. (**s'**) If the word **does not end in _s_, add '_s_** on the end of the word.

THE UBIQUITOUS BUT BELOVED COMMA

The second chunk of mechanics is the comma. There are actually only twelve rules for the student to master by middle school. My classes came up with the idea for LIST. Students must list the twelve rules to add them to the scavenger hunt.

L stands for letter. Think about the parts of a letter, and you have the first three rules: an address, a date, and the greeting and closing of a friendly letter. In my last year of teaching, only three students out of 135 could punctuate their own address correctly. Use white boards and have students write their own address. Check the room and let those who do it correctly move to the back of the room. Proceed through the rules until everyone has done each one correctly. Then pretest. It saves time.

Address: Write the examples in a sentence because you are teaching how to deal with the test or sentence structure, not envelopes. I live at 2122 Mulberry Ln., Alton, IL 60077. Go over every mark and abbreviation.

Date: On Monday, January 15, 2000, I was born. Students must begin the sentence with the prepositional phrase, not "I was born," because they will miss the comma following *2000* which is what is tested. They are setting off all items in the date, including the last item, from the sentence pattern.

Greeting and closing of a friendly letter: Dear Sam, Sincerely yours, Use *sincerely* to work on the correct spelling and two words in the closing to cover not capitalizing the second word.

I stands for introductory items and interrupters. Five rules are covered in this chunk.

Introductory words. (Yes, no, oh, well) Yes, I know the comma rules.

Introductory verbals. (Understanding the rule depends on understanding syntax. You taught verbals so this rule is not a problem and reviews verbals. Set off introductory verbals from the pattern.)
Running through the woods, the deer escaped the hunters. (participle)
To be able to edit well, students must learn the comma rules. (infinitive)
By improving students' editing skills, they gain confidence. (gerund—if the gerund is the subject and not in a prepositional phrase, it, of course, is not set off, since the parts of the pattern are not separated from one another.)

(Some texts include the introductory dependent clause here, but since punctuating these clauses results in major structural errors, the rule is better taught with a discussion of sentence types.)

Interrupters: There are three types of interrupters. These are also called parenthetical expressions, but then you have to teach the term. Save parenthetical for high school and parentheses. The three interrupters include short expressions such as *of course, in my opinion, it seems to me, however, therefore,* and appositives and nouns of address. The latter two are new to the students and require the most practice.

Interrupters: School, I think, is important. Remind students that if the sentence begins, "I think school is important," "*I think*" is the subject and verb of the pattern, and therefore, should not be set off.

Appositives: Nouns or pronouns that rename and explain the preceding noun are appositives.

School, the place where I spend most of my day, is important. Show how appositives can be short: Molly, my dog, is barking. Then show

how by extending them, the length of the sentence grows. (Remember that sentence length is a measure of mature writing.) Molly, my beloved Labrador retriever who happens to be barking unnecessarily, is disrupting my work. Show the appositive in the beginning, middle, and end of the sentence.

Nouns of address. Nouns of address indicate who or what is being spoken to.

Molly, stop barking.
Molly, my dog is barking is a very different sentence than *Molly,* my dog, *is barking.* Because of the punctuation in the second example, Molly could be a person or the dog. Have students create sentences showing the difference and effect of the comma in creating appositives and the nouns of address. The noun of address can occur in the beginning, middle, and end of a sentence.

S stands for series and separating adjectives.
Students are comfortable with saying a list of things, but items in a series suggests the distinction between two items which comprise a compound structure and no comma, or three or more items which require a comma.
I like cake, pies, and cookies. Make students put in the commas before the conjunction unless they have a specific reason to omit it.

When separating adjectives, if the student can say *and* between the two adjectives, then the comma is probably needed.

The deep, dark cave was scary. (The major error, other than omitting the mark, is to put a comma after *dark.* Do not separate an adjective from the noun it is modifying. (Ah, syntax.)

T stands, at last, for sentence types. If you have taught syntax, these rules are easily covered. There are two types of sentences requiring punctuation: the compound and the complex with an introductory adverbial dependent clause. If a teacher begins with punctuation, just the terminology alone will confuse a student. If, however, the teacher begins with syntax, then students are comfortable with these structures.

I fell, and I cried. Use a comma to separate two independent clauses joined with a coordinate conjunction: and, or, but, nor, for, yet.

I fell; I cried. Do not use a comma but a semi-colon in a compound sentence without a coordinate conjunction. (You already taught this rule, so this is review.)To use a comma, you will recall, is to write the evil comma splice or the equally wicked run-on.

[When I fell], I cried. Use a comma to set off an introductory adverbial dependent clause in a complex sentence. All of these terms have been taught. Note at this point one cause for fragment errors.

When I fell. I cried. Explain that to the writer the structure makes sense, but to the reader, who is dependent on the punctuation, the period totally interrupts the flow and, therefore, the comprehension. The reader stops at the period and has to start over.

If the adverbial clause is at the end of the sentence, I cried [when I fell], the comma is not necessary. It is interesting to note for students, that computer programs are only as correct as the programmer is. Many computer programs automatically put that last comma in which is incorrect. Students administered their pretests to the computer, and it scored a 40%.

Students will note many exceptions, especially in novels, T.V., etc. Remind them that they are learning a standard. Standards can be turned on and turned off. They are in control. When they take a test, they turn on the standard. When they text their friends, they turn it off. Discuss also how competitive the world is. Someone who learns English as a second language, learns the standard. If English is one's first language, it is essential to be equally proficient.

Thus ends two parts of mechanics: miscellaneous marks and the ubiquitous but beloved comma. Only one more punctuation problem to study, and the SUM is complete: Dialogue.

DIALOGUE: RARELY USED AND ALWAYS TESTED

All placement tests contain dialogue. Knowing how to punctuate simple dialogue will guarantee higher scores. The necessity of including this particular problem on placement tests escapes me, but the reality is that there are usually not one but several questions devoted to this problem.

Punctuating dialogue can be simplified easily if students learn to follow four simple steps.

1. Place quotation marks around the spoken words.
2. Capitalize the beginning of sentences, always at the start but not necessarily later on.
3. Separate the speaker from the quotation.
4. Place one end mark, remembering that periods and commas are inside quotation marks and questions marks and exclamation marks vary.

Practice distinguishing between direct and indirect quotations.

Sam said, "The game was very exciting." (Direct, use marks.)
Sam said that the game was very exciting. (Indirect, no marks.)

Practice indenting for new paragraphs for every change in speaker. Practice continuous dialogue so students see that the quotation marks go at the beginning and ending of the quotation, not around every sentence. Because they practice single sentences in texts, they think quotation marks go around every sentence.

"The game was very exciting. The star player was out, but I still enjoyed the game," said Sam.

Direct Quotations are the most frequently tested. Usually one part of the four steps above is missing or one set of quotation marks are omitted. Practice examples by always following in order the four parts for dialogue.

Sam said the game was exciting.

1.) Place the quotation marks. Sam said "the game was exciting"
2.) Capitalize the beginning of a sentence. Sam said "The game was exciting"
3.) Separate the speaker from the quotation. Sam said, "The game was exciting"
4.) Place an end mark. Sam said, "The game was exciting." Also practice the reversed order, "The game was exciting," said Sam.

Separated Quotations are punctuated two ways depending on sentence structure. If the separated quote is one sentence, then the marks will be a comma and a lower case letter beginning the continuation of the quote, but if the separated quote is two sentences, then the mark is a period and a capital beginning the second sentence.

"The game was exciting," said Sam, "even though our best player could not play."(One complex sentence.)
"The game was exciting," said Sam. "Our best player could not play." (Two separate sentences.)

Questions Marks and Exclamation Marks pose their own set of problems. Commas and periods are always inside the quotation marks, but question marks and exclamation marks go inside, between, and outside of the quotation marks depending on the sentence structure. Testing is usually pretty simple addressing only that a question mark is necessary, but teach all of the possible situations.

If the quotation is the question, the question mark is inside the quotation marks.

Sam asked, "Was the game exciting?"

If the sentence is the question, the mark is outside the quotation marks.

Did Sam say, "That game was exciting"?

Single Quotation Marks are the final problem with quotation marks. Since titles are sometimes in quotation marks, if they occur within a dialogue, they require single quotation marks.

The teacher said, "Read 'The Tell-Tale Heart' for tomorrow."
Single quotes are necessary if another quote occurs in the quote.

The teacher said, "Sam said, 'The game was exciting.'"

It gets a little messy when a question or an exclamation occurs, but if the four steps are followed, nothing is forgotten.
The teacher asked who said the game was exciting

The teacher asked, "Who said, 'The game was exciting'?" (The teacher's words are the quotation so the question mark is between the single and double quotation marks.)

Did the teacher ask who said the game was exciting

Did the teacher ask, "Who said, 'The game was exciting'"? (The sentence is the question so the question mark is at the end of the sentence. Note that only one end mark is used.)

The teacher smiled and said Sam questioned what is the assignment

The teacher smiled and said, "Sam questioned, 'What is the assignment?'"(Sam's comment is the question so the question mark goes inside the single quote.)

And that's it! The SUM of all those errors is mastered. Having the class create the examples eliminates texts, allows for group work, and reteaches concepts as students create examples and share them. The entire "scavenger hunt" fits on four sheets to give to students as a guide after direct instruction. If students create a notebook of concepts and practice, they have their own text for years to come. The practice continues all through school and life; a reference manual that they create is an invaluable tool.

Just one quick note about capitalization. Given that the media ignores it, and students are texting without using it, this particular skill is headed for trouble. However, at the time of this writing, students learn almost all of the capitalization rules from their diligent K-5 teachers. By middle school the only problems are listed at the end of the Scavenger List for Editing.

I sincerely hope that you have found this information helpful. Best wishes in your teaching/student endeavors and may you enjoy the art of language.

THE SUM SCAVENGER LIST
FOR EDITING

Syntax

Analyze the sentence structure to correct Fragments, Comma Splices, and Run-ons and to improve sentence variety.

Usage

Subject-Verb Agreement Rule: A singular subject takes a singular verb, and singular verbs end in *s*.

Find the subject and the verb. Apply the rule.

Beware: Prepositional phrases (The objects are never subjects.)

Indefinite pronouns (They have a problem with number.)
Compound subjects (If joined by *and*, the subjects are plural; if joined by *or* or *nor,* the verb agrees with the closer subject.

Pronouns: Case, Agreement, and Reference (CAR) Rule: A pronoun agrees with its antecedent in person, number, and gender. The case is determined by the sentence part.

Identify the pronoun. (Relative, Interrogative, Demonstrative, Indefinite, and Personal).

1.) Reference: Make certain the pronoun has an antecedent (especially *it* and *this)*

2.) Agreement: Memorize the pronoun chart to apply it.

Personal Pronouns

Person	Nominative Case		Objective Case		Possessive Case	
	S	Pl	S	Pl	S	Pl
1st	I	we	me	us	my	our
2nd	you	you	you	you	your	your
3rd	he, she, it	they	him, her, it	them	his, her its	their

Find the pronoun and its antecedent.

Determine the person, number, and gender of both and make sure they are the same.

Beware: Indefinite pronouns and compound subjects.

3.) Case: Remember that nominative case pronouns are subjects and predicate nouns. Objective case pronouns are direct objects, indirect objects, and objects of prepositions.

Find the pronoun.

Determine the sentence part.

Choose the appropriate form of the pronoun by applying the pronoun chart. The pronouns *I, you, he, she, it, we, you, they* will be subjects and predicate nouns; the pronouns *me, you, him, her, it, us, you them* will be objects.

Verbs Rule: Choose the appropriate principal part for the tense needed. Know that all verbs have four principal parts and that the present principal part forms present and future tense, the past principal part forms past tense, and the past participle principal part forms all three perfect tenses with an auxiliary verb.

Auxiliary or helping verbs indicate tense. (Shall, will—future; has, have—present perfect; had—past perfect; shall have, will have—future perfect

Principal Parts

Present	Past	Past Participle
sing	sang	sung

Tense

Present	Past	Future	Present Perfect	Past Perfect	Future Perfect
sing	sang	will sing	has sung	had sung	will have sung

Find the verb.

Determine the tense.

Choose the appropriate principal part for the tense.

Study lie, lay, lain; lay, laid, laid; burst, burst, burst; bring, brought, brought

Modifiers

Beware: Good (adjective) and Well (adverb)
    Double Negatives (*hardly* and *scarcely* are negatives)

Comparisons:

Use er or *more* for comparing two items.
Use *est* or *most* for comparing three or more items.

Never use *er* and *more* or *est* and *most* in the same comparison. (The dictionary gives the comparisons for irregular modifiers using *more* or *most*.)

Mechanics

Miscellaneous Marks (6 marks)

(:) colon—(2:00 P.M.   Dear Sir: Items to follow: Do not separate predicates (verbs) from their direct objects with a colon.

(;) semi-colon—(compound sentences without a coordinate conjunction, *and, or, but, nor, for.* Beware of *therefore, however,* etc. These words are not coordinate conjunctions but interrupters.

(-) hyphen—(twenty-one to ninety-nine and fractions used as adjectives not nouns)

(___ " ")—underlining and quotation marks (underline or use italics, not both at the same time) for long works and quotation marks for short works plus art work, trains, ships, and aircraft)

(') apostrophe—

Singular Nouns	Singular Possessive	Plural Nouns	Plural Possessive
girl	girl 's	girls	girls '
child	child 's	children	children 's

For singular possessive, write the singular form of the noun and add *'s*.

For plural possessive, write the plural form. Look at the ending. If the word ends in *s*, add *'s*; if the word does not end in *s*, add *s'*.

The Ubiquitous, Beloved Comma LIST

L (letter):   **address** I live at 3222 N. Ave., Antioch, IL 60045.

date   On Monday, October 1, 2005, I was born.
greeting and **closing** of a friendly letter Dear Sam, Sincerely yours,

I (introductory):   **introductory words** yes, no, oh, well
introductory verbals   Speaking in a low voice,
the girl began her speech.
(interrupters): **interrupters** (parenthetical expressions) I think,
it seems to me, in my opinion
appositives My dog, Molly, is a black lab.
nouns of address Molly, fetch your duck.

S (**series**) We enjoy eating fruits, vegetables, and sweet treats.
(**separate adjectives**) The cold, dark cave frightened the children.

T (types of sentences) **compound sentence with a coordinate conjunction: and, or, but, nor, for, yet** <u>I cry</u>, and <u>I laugh</u>. <u>I cry and laugh</u>. Know the difference.

complex sentence with an introductory
adverbial dependent clause [Although it
looks like rain], <u>we are still having
a picnic</u>.

Dialogue

Direct Quote: **"I** like syntax," said Sam.
Divided Quote: **"I** like syntax," said Sam, "and I think it is easy."
"I like syntax," said Sam. "Yesterday I got a
perfect score on my ACT."

Quotation with a Question/Exclamation: **"D**o you like syntax?**"** asked Sam**.** (Note that the separation between the quote and the speaker is NOT a comma.)

Sam asked**, "D**o you like syntax?**"**

Follow the four steps: Quotation marks, capitalization or not, separate the quote from the speaker, end mark.

Quote within a quote: **"P**lease read**,** 'The Raven,**'"** said the teacher**.**

Commas and periods go inside the quotation marks; question marks and exclamation points vary according to syntax.

Capitalization: (most commonly missed and tested) summer, fall, winter, spring, autumn (no seasons); algebra, language arts, chemistry, **A**lgebra I, **C**hemistry II (only subjects followed by a number); north, south (not directions); **N**orth, **S**outh (geographic locations); **G**erman shepherd**, F**ord truck (proper noun not the common noun)

A Summary of the Most Important Points for Memorization

(You need to chant these while taking attendance or set to music or some sort of rhythm. Do whatever it takes to achieve retention.)

The Syntax Chart terms and definitions.

The coordinate conjunctions: and, or, but, nor, for, yet.

The verbs that are almost always the predicate or part of it: may, might; shall, should; will, would; can, could; do, did, done; has, have, had; am, is, was, were; be, being, been.

Usage Rules:

A pronoun agrees with its antecedent in person, number, and gender. The case is determined by the sentence part.

Personal Pronouns Nominative Case: I, you, he, she, it, we, you, they

A singular subject takes a singular verb, and singular verbs end in s.

Tests should not be just about correctly editing errors.

Design pretests, practice, and posttests about the scavenger list of possible errors. The students have to know what they are looking for to score high. It is not a guessing game. Tests cover the SUM. The better the students are at systematically running though syntax or sentence errors, four usage problems, six miscellaneous marks, the comma, dialogue, and a bit of capitalization the greater the success.

Good test takers take the offense. They analyze the test—knowing exactly what is going to be asked. They are on a scavenger hunt, and this hunting skill will serve them the rest of their lives as they expertly and confidently edit their speaking and writing endeavors.

A Review for Mastering Syntax

Level I: Memorize the chart. The student is able to reproduce the chart from memory. Students know the five categories with the appropriate terms arranged and spelled correctly.

Level II: Memorize the definitions for each term including phrase and clause. Definitions need to be exact.

Level III: Identify the various terms in sentences.

Level IV: Give an example of each term in an original sentence.

When Levels I and II are mastered, the students begins work on Level III in the following order:

Parts of a Sentence. The objective is to recognize the syntactic patterns S+V, S + V + DO, S + V+ IO + DO, S + V+ PN (PA/PP) phrases. Because of the frequency of the prepositional phrase, mastering it early facilitates the rest of the process. However, the prepositional phrase can be taught later, but if so, the phrase is omitted from examples until covered.

Parts of Speech. The sentence patterns are always marked first in every sentence. Then the parts of speech are labeled. The instruction on the parts of speech focuses on the noun functioning as a S, DO, IO, PN, or OP (object of a preposition) NOT on whether one is dealing with a person, place, or thing. A noun is the name of an idea that fills a slot in a sentence.

The verb makes up the predicate. The correct term for the sentence part is predicate, but since all predicates are verbs, for convenience in labeling, we call the predicate the verb in the sentence. Four verbs may comprise the predicate such as *should have been studying.*

The preposition is already in place after the prepositional phrase has be taught.

The conjunction is introduced as a coordinate conjunction: and, or, but, nor, for, yet. (There are correlative conjunctions either/or, neither/nor, not only/but also, but they are not significant in testing.)

The remaining two parts of speech, the adjective and the adverb, are modifiers. After the student has labeled all of the sentence parts and put a line through the prepositional phrases, the student identifies the modifiers by asking what word in the sentence they affect. For example, an adjective affects a noun in some way; therefore, the word affecting the noun is an adjective.

Phrases: The phrases are introduced next. The verbals are the heart of good writing and development.

Clauses: Once all of the pieces are covered, the clause is introduced.

Sentence Types: Finally, the concept of a sentence with all of the puzzle pieces is in place.

Steps for Analyzing Syntax

1. Find the verb.

2. Know that a linking verb links S + PN, PA, PP, and an action verb is followed by a DO or IO + DO.

3. Say to yourself, "Who or what" and read the verb and the rest of the sentence.

Example: The girl wrote a letter to her friend in Europe.

> 1. The verb is *wrote*.
> 2. *Wrote* is an action verb; therefore, IF there is a complement, a DO or a PN, it will be a DO.
> 3. Who or what wrote the letter to her friend in Europe? *Girl.*
> 4. Now finish the pattern. Read the subject and the verb and ask what? The girl wrote what? *Letter.* The answer to the question is the complement.

$$S \ + \ V \ + \ DO$$
girl| wrote| letter

Example: The tree has many dry leaves on its limbs.

> 1. The verb is *has*.
> 2. The verb is action; therefore, the complement, if there is one will be a DO.
> 3. Who or what has many dry leaves on its limbs? *Tree.*
> 4. The tree has what? *Leaves.*

S + V + DO
<u>tree| has| leaves</u>

5. Now follow the flow chart. You have memorized a chart of syntactic structures. Now you must apply what you have memorized to the sentence for analysis.

Ask yourself what words are left in the sentence: many, dry, on, its, limbs.

6. Follow the steps: Analyze.

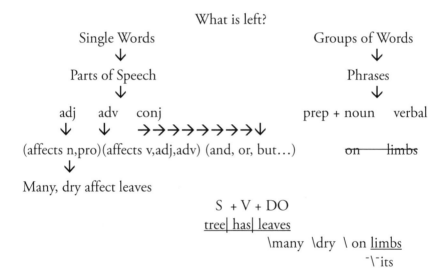

Level III Practice: Identifying the Parts of a Sentence to recognize the pattern in all English sentences.

1. S + V: Dogs bark.
              Are you leaving?
              Stop.

Always find the verb first. *Bark.*

Then say, "Who or what (verb)? Who or what barks? *Dogs.*

Label the sentence above the word so that the pattern is obvious.

S + V
Dogs bark.

Make questions statements. Are you leaving? You are leaving.

What is the verb? *Are leaving.*

Who or what are leaving? *You.*

S + V
You are leaving.

Commands have the understood subject *You.*

What is the verb? *Stop.*

Who or what stops? *You.*

S + V
X (you) stop

A pattern may have two or more subjects and verbs. These are compound and labeled the same.

Dolphins and whales leap and swim.

What is the verb(s)? *Leap, swim.*

Who or what leap and swim? *Dolphins, whales.*

S   +   V
Dolphins and whales leap and swim.

The above sentence illustrates that the number of subjects and verbs does not determine the pattern. The order creates the pattern, and there is only one order here so there is only one pattern.

1. Max left.
2. Jesse is studying.
3. Watch.
4. Should you have been working?
5. Molly and Roy laughed and played.

Once the basic pattern, S + V, is mastered, additional sentence parts are added.

2. S + V + DO: We like pizza.

The direct object follows an action verb and receives the action.

What is the verb? *Like.*

Who or what likes pizza? *We.*

Now say the subject plus the verb and ask what.

We like what? *Pizza;* therefore, pizza is the direct object. Test by asking if the pizza is what is liked.

S + V + DO
We like pizza.

Birds eat bugs and worms.

What is the verb? Eat.

Who or what eats bugs and worms? Birds.

Birds eat what? Bugs and worms.

There is a compound direct object (two or more objects) but still only one pattern.

S + V + DO
Birds eat bugs and worms.

Practice:

1. The business bought the computer.
2. He sent clothes.
3. Jesse drew a picture.
4. Max and Duke are hunting ducks.
5. Max and Duke are hunting ducks and catching fish. (Hunting has a DO, ducks, and catching has a DO, fish; however, there is still only one pattern.)

```
S   +   V   +   DO
Max |  are hunting |  ducks
 a        a
 n  > <   n
 d        d
Duke |  catching   |  fish
```

3. S + V + IO + DO: The business bought the school a computer.

The indirect object receives the direct object. The indirect object is always in front of the direct object.

What is the verb? *Bought.*

Who or what bought the school a computer? *Business.*

The business bought what? *Computer.*

Now ask, who received the computer? *School.* (The indirect object receives the direct object; the school receives the computer.)

Practice:

1. He sent the American Red Cross and Goodwill Industries the equipment.
2. The mother gave the baby and the puppies toys.
3. Jesse drew her mother a picture.
4. Max gave the dog a treat.
5. Jenny gave the singers and the dancers cues.

The predicate nouns, predicate adjectives, and predicate pronouns are the same structures except different parts of speech. The predicate "somethings" follow linking verbs and rename or describe the subject. There is no action verb.

Barbra Streisand is a singer.

She is old.

The victim is he.

What is the verb? *Is* (a linking verb) Who or what is a singer? *Barbra Streisand*, Who or what is *old*? She. Who or what is he? Victim. Barbra Streisand is what? *Singer*. She is what? *Old*. The victim is what? *He*.

S + V; S + V +DO; S + V + IO + DO; S + V + PN (PA/PP) are the basic syntactic patterns and must be mastered to proceed further. The direct object, indirect object, predicate noun, predicate pronoun, and predicate adjective are called complements because they complete the meaning of the pattern.

Once the basic patterns are mastered, students begin Parts of Speech and prepositional phrases. Prepositional phrases can be delayed until the Phrase section of the chart, but then none should be included in examples before then.

Label the Parts of Speech of the Sentence Parts first. S, DO, IO, PN, PA, PP are labeled first. Nouns are subjects and objects and predicate nouns. Pronouns are the same as well as predicate pronouns. Adjectives are predicate adjectives.

The young, energetic child played with the skateboard.

What is the verb? *Played*.

Who or what played with the skateboard? *Child*. (Always say the words following the verb when looking for the subject.)

Now ask, "What is left?" Two possibilities exist: single words that will be parts of speech and grouping of words which go together in a unit which will be a phrase.

What is left? *Soft, silky,* and *with a shoelace*.

Now ask of all the single words, "What is _____ doing in the sentence?" What is *soft* doing in the sentence? What is it affecting? *Soft* affects kitten. *Kitten* is a noun; therefore, *soft* is an adjective because adjectives affect nouns.

What is *silky* doing in the sentence? *Silky* is affecting kitten. *Kitten* is a noun; therefore, *silky* is an adjective because and adjective affects a noun.

What is left? The group of words *with a shoelace*. A group of words by definition is a phrase. Therefore, *with a shoelace* is a phrase. There are two types of phrases: prepositional or verbal depending on the first word. (usually) If the first word is a preposition, the phrase is a prepositional phrase; if the first word is a verb, it is a verbal phrase. *With* is not a verb; therefore, *with a shoelace* is a prepositional phrase beginning with the prep, *with*, and ending with a noun, *shoelace*.

Think of the chart for phrases and clauses as outlines of the puzzle pieces and a flow chart for analyzing the sentence.

Once a group of words is identified as a verbal, it is one of three kinds: a *participle* if it acts like an adjective, an infinitives if it begins with *to + verb* and acts like a noun, adjective, or adverb, or a *gerund* if it ends in *ing* and acts like a noun.

After identifying all of the puzzle pieces, look at the entire pattern with all of its modifying parts of speech and phrases. If the pattern is a complete thought, the clause is independent; and incomplete thought is the dependent clause, one of three types: noun, adjective, or adverb depending on how the entire clause functions in the sentence.

Sentence types are just the number and combination of the independent and dependent clauses.

S   +   V   +   PA   S +   S +

[Although studying syntax seems complicated], <u>students</u> [who finally

s.conj   n   v   adj   n   r.pro adv

V +   DO   V   S + V   + DO

master the concept] <u>score very well ~~on tests~~</u>, and <u>they write a greater variety</u>

  v   n   v   adv   adv   pro   v   adj   n

~~of sentence structures.~~

Although studying syntax seems complicated, students who finally master the concept score very well on tests, and they write a greater variety of sentence structures.

What are the verbs: *seems, master, score, write*

Do each pattern around these verbs.

Who or what seems complicated? *Studying syntax* (the gerund phrase)

Studying syntax seems what? *Complicated.*

What's left? *Although* (a subordinate conjunction; subordinate conjunctions introduce adverbial clauses)

Does *Although studying syntax seems complicated* stand alone? No, because it is an introductory adverbial dependent clause. Enclose in brackets and circle the gerund phrase.

Remember students memorize the relative pronouns *who, whom, whose, which,* and *that.* They have some difficulty at first seeing *who* as the subject of master, but once they have practiced, they pick out adjective dependent clauses without any trouble.

What is the verb? *Master.*

Who masters the concept? *Who,* the relative pronoun which refers to the students and means the students.

Who master what? *Concept.*

What's left? *Finally. Finally* affects *master* a verb; therefore, *finally* is an adverb.

Does the clause *who finally master the concept* stand alone? No, it is dependent. Enclose in brackets.

What type of dependent clause? What is the clause affecting? The clause affects the noun *students;* therefore, the dependent clause is an adjective dependent clause.

What is the verb? *Score.*

Who scores well on tests? *Students*

Students score what? Not how, but what? No answer. The pattern is S + V.

What's left? *Well,* ~~on tests~~. *Well* is affecting *score; score* is a verb; adverbs affect verbs; therefore, *well* is an adverb. *On tests* is a group of words; therefore, a phrase, one of two kinds: prepositional or verbal. *On* is not a verb; therefore, *on tests* is a prepositional phrase.

Does the clause stand alone? Yes, this is the independent clause that made the sentence. Underline the independent clause.

What is the verb? *Write.*

Who writes a greater variety of sentence structures? *They.*

They write what? *Variety.*

What's left? *Greater, of sentence structures. Greater* affects *variety; variety* is a noun; therefore, *greater* is an adjective. Of sentence structures is a group of words; therefore, *of sentence structures* is a phrase, one of two kinds: prepositional or verbal. *Of* is not a verb; therefore, *of sentence structures* is a prepositional phrase.

Does the clause stand alone? Yes. The pattern is an independent clause. Underline the independent clause.

Since there are two independent clauses and at least one dependent clause, this sentence is compound complex.

The only word not accounted for is and, the coordinate conjunction joining the two independent clauses. Coordinate conjunctions join words, phrases, and in this case, clauses. Students have already memorized the conjunctions; they need only analyze what the conjunctions are joining. Then, looking at the structures that are joined, if they are the same, they are parallel. If not, the sentence needs to be rewritten. Parallelism is easy to teach, if students understand syntax, and parallelism is tested.

When students can analyze a sentence as illustrated, they can understand their own style of writing. They are now empowered to evaluate their writing.

Level IV: Comprehending Syntax

In order to comprehend syntax, students must be able to operate on Level IV with the terms. Level IV is being able to create original structures for every term in the chart. Students should be able to do the following:

1. Write a simple sentence.
   <u>I walked to my friend's house</u>. (one pattern)

2. Write a simple sentence with a compound verb.
   <u>I walked to my friend's house and played in the yard</u>. (one pattern)

3. Write a compound sentence two ways and punctuate both correctly.
   <u>I walked to my friend's house</u>, **and** <u>we played in the yard</u>. (two patterns)
   <u>I walked to my friend's house</u>; <u>we played in the yard</u>. (two patterns)

4. Write a complex sentence with an introductory adverbial dependent clause and punctuate correctly.
   [When I walked to my friend's house,] we played in the yard.

5. Write a complex sentence with an adverbial dependent clause at the end of the sentence and punctuate correctly.
   We played in the yard [*when I walked to my friend's house*].

6. Write a complex sentence with an adjective clause in the middle of the independent clause.
   My friend, [*who likes to play in the yard*], lives down the street.

7. Write a complex sentence with an adjective clause at the end of the sentence.
   I played in the yard with my friend, [*who lives down the street*].

8. Write a complex sentence with a noun clause embedded in the independent clause as the subject.

[*That I have a friend*] makes me happy.

9. Write an embedded noun clause as the direct object in the independent clause.

I said [*that my friend and I played in the yard.*]

10. Write an embedded noun clause as the predicate noun in the independent clause.

Our favorite activity is [*that my friend and I play in the yard*].

11. Write a noun clause as the object of a preposition.

The parents were looking for *who left the gate open.*

12. Write a sentence with an introductory participial phrase punctuated correctly.

Playing in the yard, my friend and I forgot to eat lunch.

13. Write and punctuate sentences with infinitive phrases as nouns, adjectives, and adverbs.

To play in the yard, my friend and I had to wait for good weather.
The teacher *to ask about syntax* is down the hall.
The children were running *to play in the yard.*

14. Write gerund phrases in each of the noun positions of a sentence.

Playing in the yard is fun. (S)
We like *playing in the yard.* (DO)
Our favorite pastime is *playing in the yard.* (PN)
I am writing ~~about *playing in the yard*~~. (OP)

APPENDIX I

The Syntax Chart

Parts of Speech

noun
pronoun
verb
conjunction
interjection
preposition
adjective
adverb

Definitions:
noun - names
pronoun - takes the place of a noun
verb- shows action or links
conjunction - joins words, phrases, and clauses
interjection - shows emotion
preposition - shows a relationship between a noun or pronoun and the rest of the sentence
adjective - modifies nouns and pronouns
adverb - modifies verbs, adjectives, and other adverbs

coordinate conjunctions:
and, or, but, nor, for, yet

subordinate conjunctions: if, since, when, because

relative pronouns: who, whom, whose, which, that

Parts of a Sentence

subject
verb
direct object
indirect object
predicate noun
predicate adjective

subject - who or what does the action or is linked
verb - shows action or is linked
direct object - receives the action
indirect object - receives the direct object
predicate noun - follows a linking verb and renames the subject
predicate adjective - follows a linking verb and describes the subject

linking verbs:
am   was   be
are   were   been
is   become

helping verbs:
do   have   may
did   has   might
does   had   must

could   can
would   will
should   shall

Phrases
(a group of words)

prepositional
verbal
participle
infinitive
gerund

prepositional - prep + noun
verbal - verb that acts like a noun, adjective, or adverb
participle - verb that acts like an adjective
infinitive - to + a verb that acts like a noun, adjective, or adverb
gerund - verb ending in ing that acts like a noun

Clauses
(group of words with a subject and a verb)

independent
dependent
noun
adjective
adverb

independent - a complete idea
dependent - an incomplete idea
noun - acts like a noun
adjective - acts like an adjective
adverb - acts like an adverb

Sentence Types

simple
compound
complex

simple - 1 independent clause
compound - 2 or more independent clauses
complex - an independent plus a dependent clause

Patterns:

S + V
S + V + DO
S + V + IO + DO
S + V + PN (PP)
S + V + PA

Punctuation Rules:

1. Use a semicolon, or use a comma with a coordinate conjunction in a compound sentence.
2. Use a comma to set off an introductory adverbial dependent clause in a complex sentence.

APPENDIX II

Vocabulary Continuum

An Evaluation of My Progress

	I can spell the word and put it in the correct category	I know the the definition	I can find the word in a sentence	I can make my own example
Parts of Speech				
noun				
pronoun				
verb				
conjunction				
interjection				
preposition				
adjective				
adverb				
Parts of a Sentence				
subject				
verb				
direct object				
indirect object				
predicate noun				
predicate adjective				
Phrases				
phrase				
prepositional				
verbal				
participle				
infinitive				
gerund				
Clauses				
clause				
independent				
dependent				
noun clause				
adjective clause				
adverb clause				
Sentence Types				
simple				
compound				
complex				
complements				
coordinate conjunctions				
subordinate conjunctions				
relative pronouns				

APPENDIX III

Syntax Flow Chart

Work the Puzzle
Find the Patterns:
S+V, S+V+DO, S+V+IO+DO
S+V=PN,PA,PP

Identify the verb
-action or linking-

Find the Subject
"Who or what say the verb
and the rest of
sentence"
S + V

Say the S + V
what?

No answer
(S + V)

ACTION

LINKING

What is left?

Nothing

Direct Object
receives the <u>action</u>
(S + V + DO)

Predicate Noun
Follows a <u>linking</u> verb and
renames the subject
(S + V + PN, PA, PP)

S + V

Indirect Object
receives the
direct object
(S + V + IO + DO)

Predicate Adjective
Follows a linking verb and
describes the subject
(S + V + PA, PP)

No

Is there more than
one pattern?

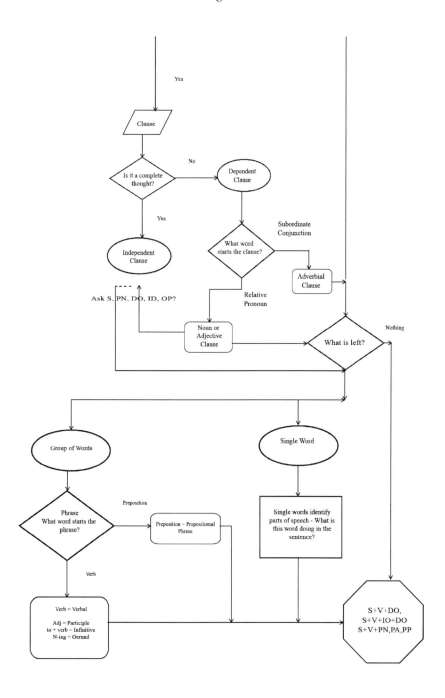

Sources

English Journal. "Revitalizing Grammar." Volume 92, No. 3, January 2003.

The entire journal is dedicated to understanding syntax and the ongoing controversy regarding instruction. The NCTE has not, as far as I am aware, recanted its position, but this issue supports all of the reasons why it should. Consider the controversy between whole language and phonics. Phonics was thrown out (the baby with the water), but now educators agree that reading instruction is a combination of approaches not one or the other. The same is true of syntax instruction.

Fromkin, Victoria and Rodman, Robert. *An Introduction to Language.* Harcourt Brace College Publications, 1974. ISBN: 0-03-054983-3.

A linguistics text.

Given, Barbara K. *Teaching to the Brain's Natural Learning Systems.* ADCD 2002. ISBN: 0-87120-569-6.

Organizes brain research into learning systems for application in the classroom. Although the book is not related to editing skills, it is a must read for teachers and learners.

Hunt, K.W. "Grammatical Structures Written in Three Grade Levels." *NCTE Research Report No. 3.* Champaign, IL NCTE, 1965, ED 113 735.

Hunt's research is the theoretical basis for analysis of mature syntactic structures.

Pinker, Steven. *The Language Instinct.* William Morrow Company, 1994. ISBN: 0-06-097651-9.

An original and entertaining theory of linguistics and humanity containing a thorough explanation of slots in a sentence.

Pirsig, Robert M. *Zen and the Art of Motorcycle Maintenance.* William Morrow and Company, 1974. ISBN: 0-553-27747-2

The cover states the text is "an inquiry into values." I see it as a definition of excellence which is applicable to all of our endeavors—especially teaching. Pirsig argues that excellence is not a product but a moment in time when science and art come together. This book is all science, but excellence cannot be attained without it.

"Research on Composing and the Teaching of Writing." Educational Leadership, April 1987.

A summation of George Hillocks' research. (George Hillocks MetaAnalysis of Grammar Instruction.) In my opinion, the research shows how not to teach "grammar," not that skills should not be taught.